Life's Dream

Life's Dream

CLAIRE YAFFA

With an introduction by Gordon Parks

For Jim -
with wishes for you life's dream

Sincerely,
Claire Yaffa

1-19-07

RUDER FINN PRESS

Editorial Director: Susan Slack
Creative Director: Lisa Gabbay
Art Director: Sal Catania
Design Director: Emily Korsmo, Ruder Finn Design
Production Director: Valerie Thompson
Pre-Press: Steve Moss

ISBN 10: 1-932646-27-2
ISBN 13: 978-1-932646-27-6

PRINTED IN THE UNITED STATES OF AMERICA
by Ruder Finn Printing Services, New York
Bryan D'Orazio, Senior Vice President

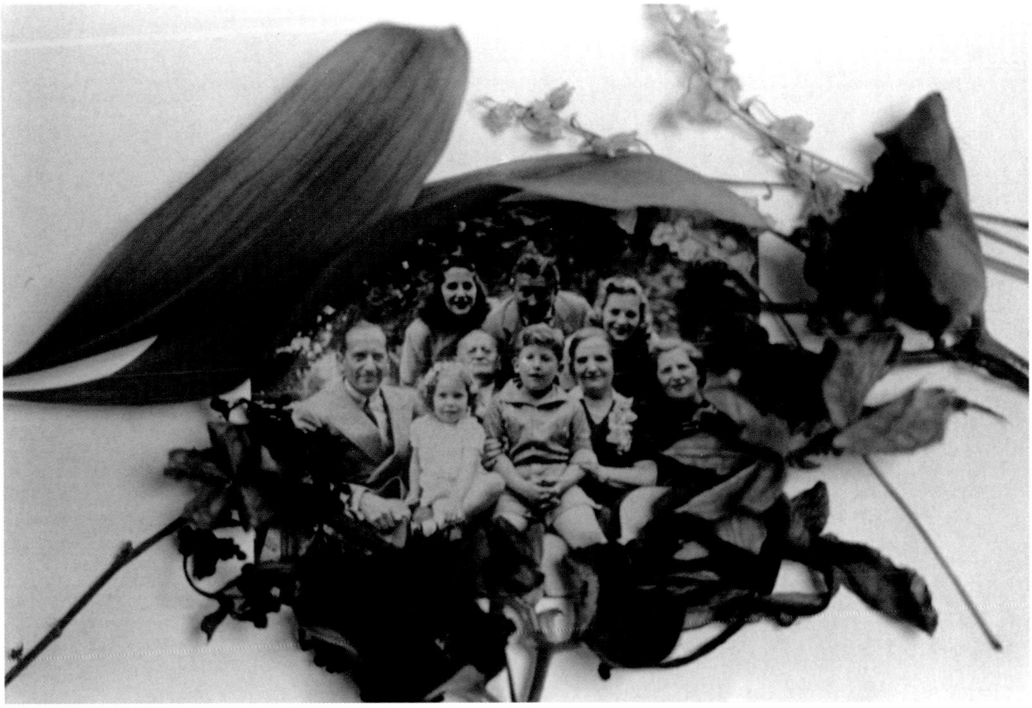

For my dear family
those who are no more
and the treasures
who remain

Introduction

by Gordon Parks

An exotic kinship of photography, art and poetry flows through Claire Yaffa's camera like one lovely stream. With her thoughts roaming the past, present and future, her eyes look searchingly toward those radiant things that refused to go away. Her camera seems to say, "Look at this. Now look at that, before they depart." Hunting recognition, invaders seem to grow in her hands—no matter that they existed yesterday, or were born today. All beautiful women and children seem to have been gently dustied with snowflakes. And the menfolk looked to have come face to face with life's toughest years. These images have been waiting for you. When Claire Yaffa knocked on the publisher's door he was waiting. And another beautiful book was about to be born. The warmth in her poetry, lending solace to the imagery, is there—all there. The waiting was worth it.

Life's Dream

Our dream of life will end, as dreams do

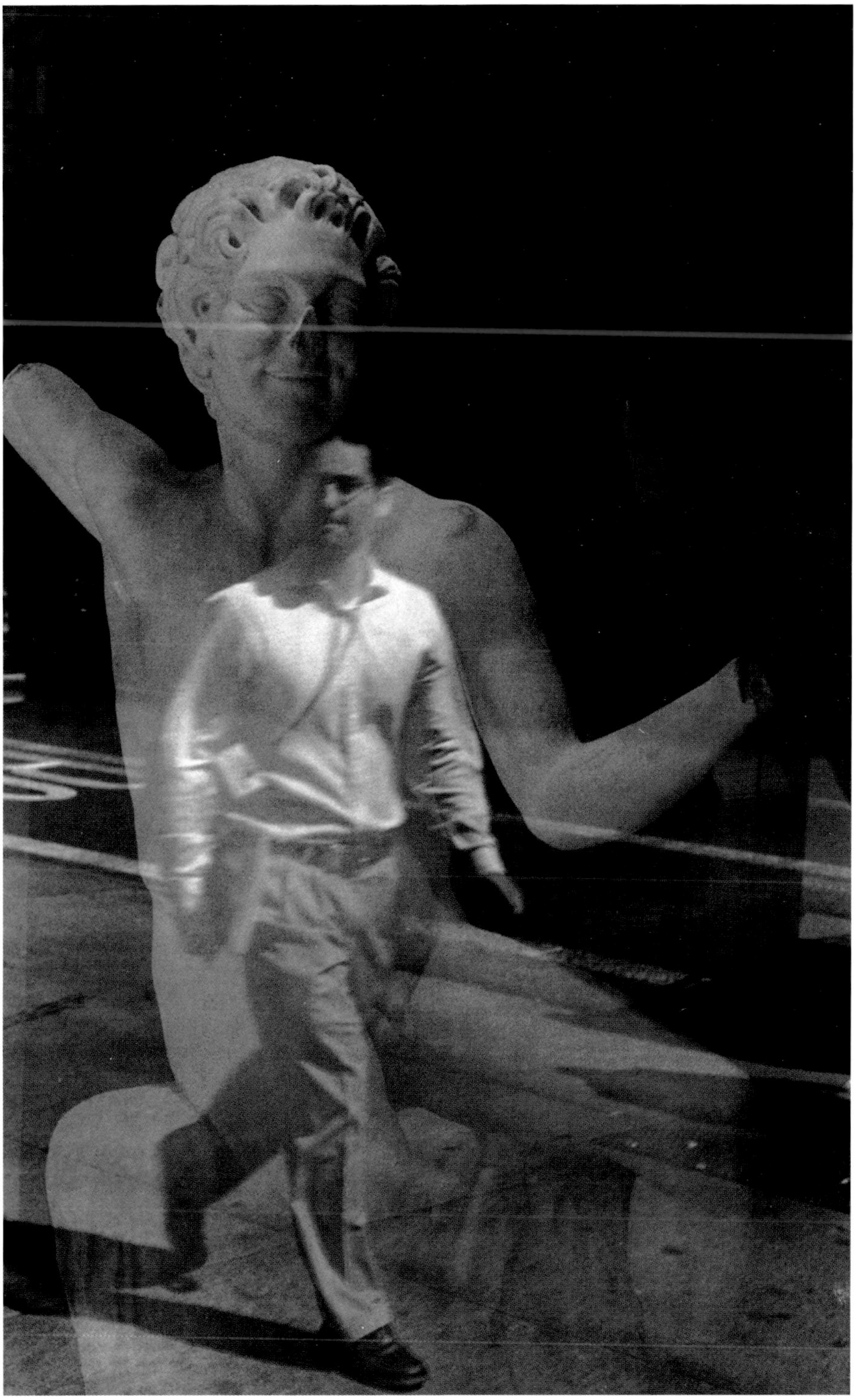

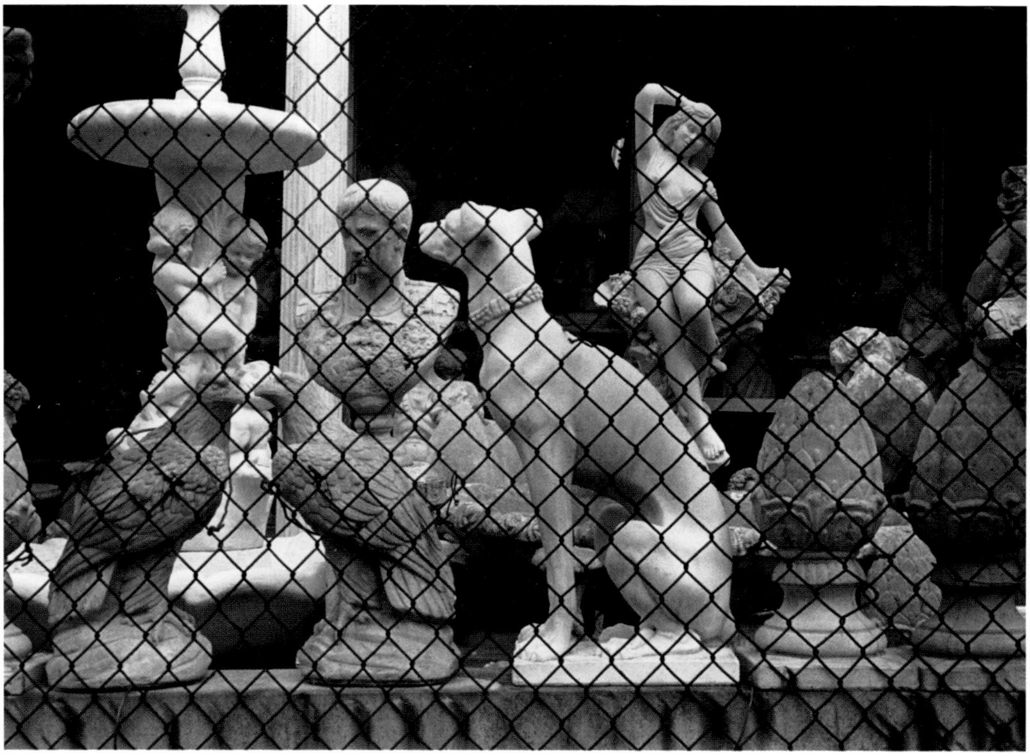

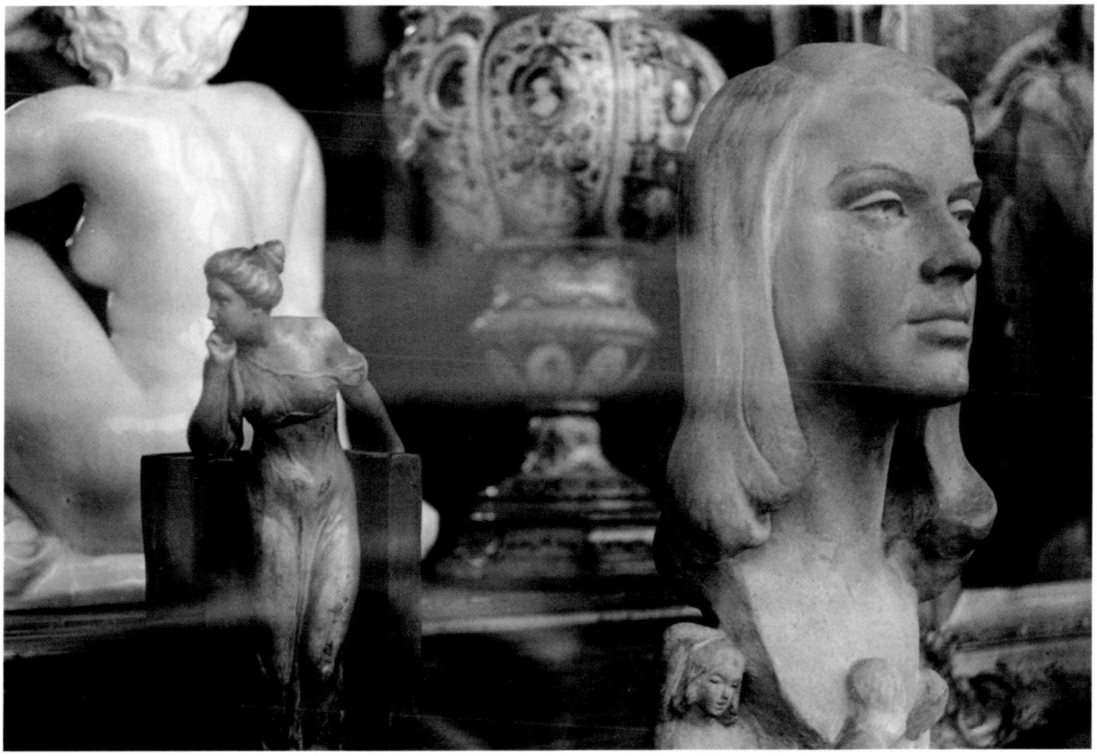

a flower lasting a short time before a petal falls
leaves touching before breaking apart

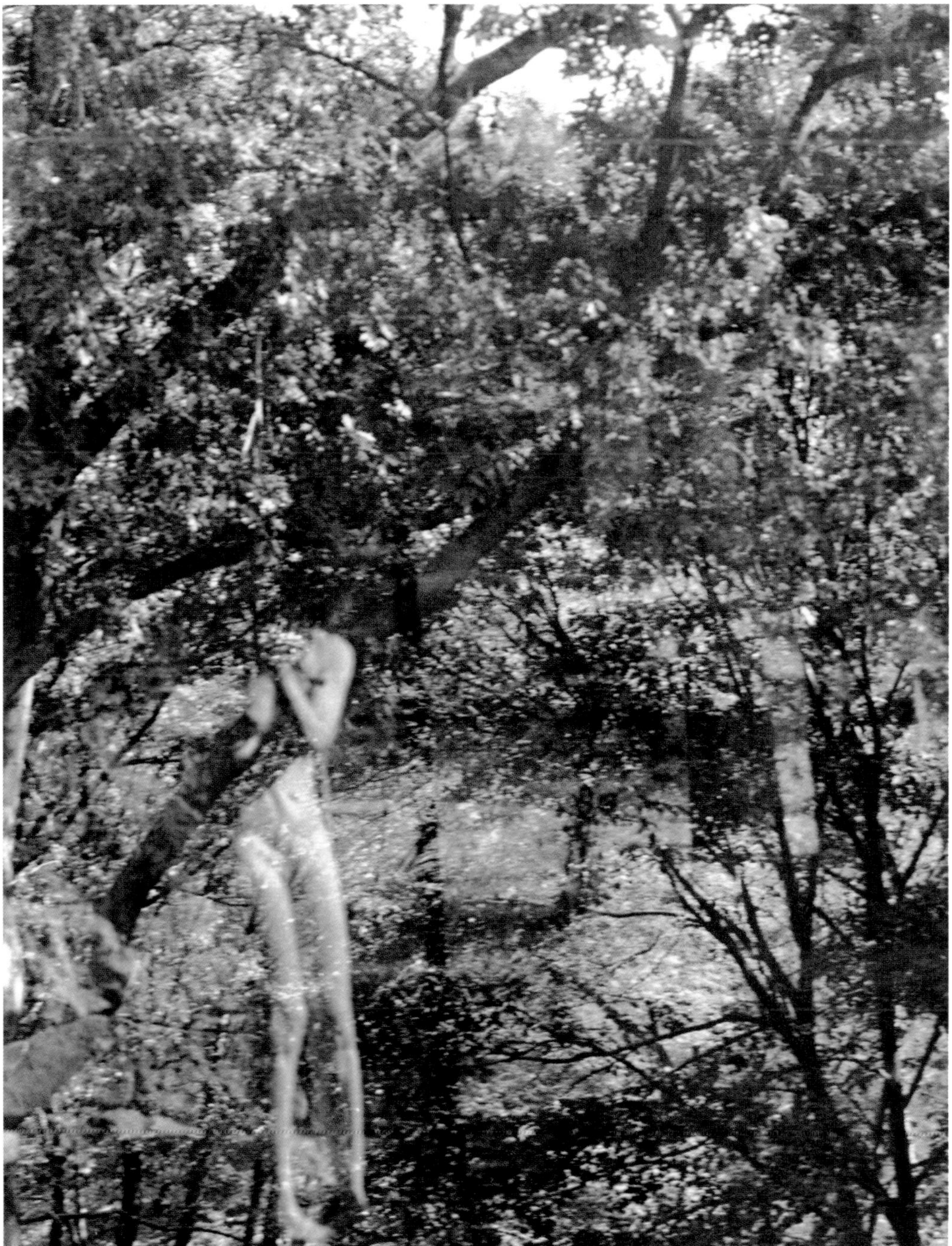

embraced by the wind
whispering who we are

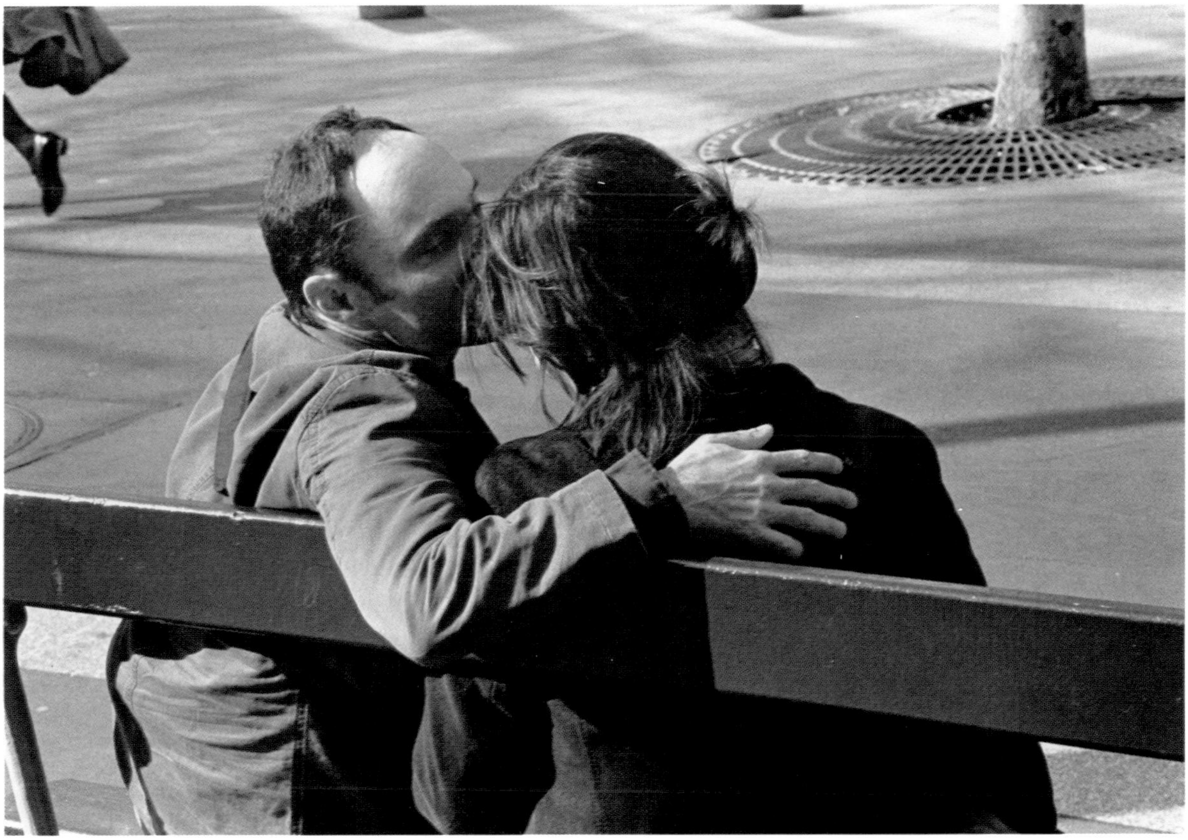

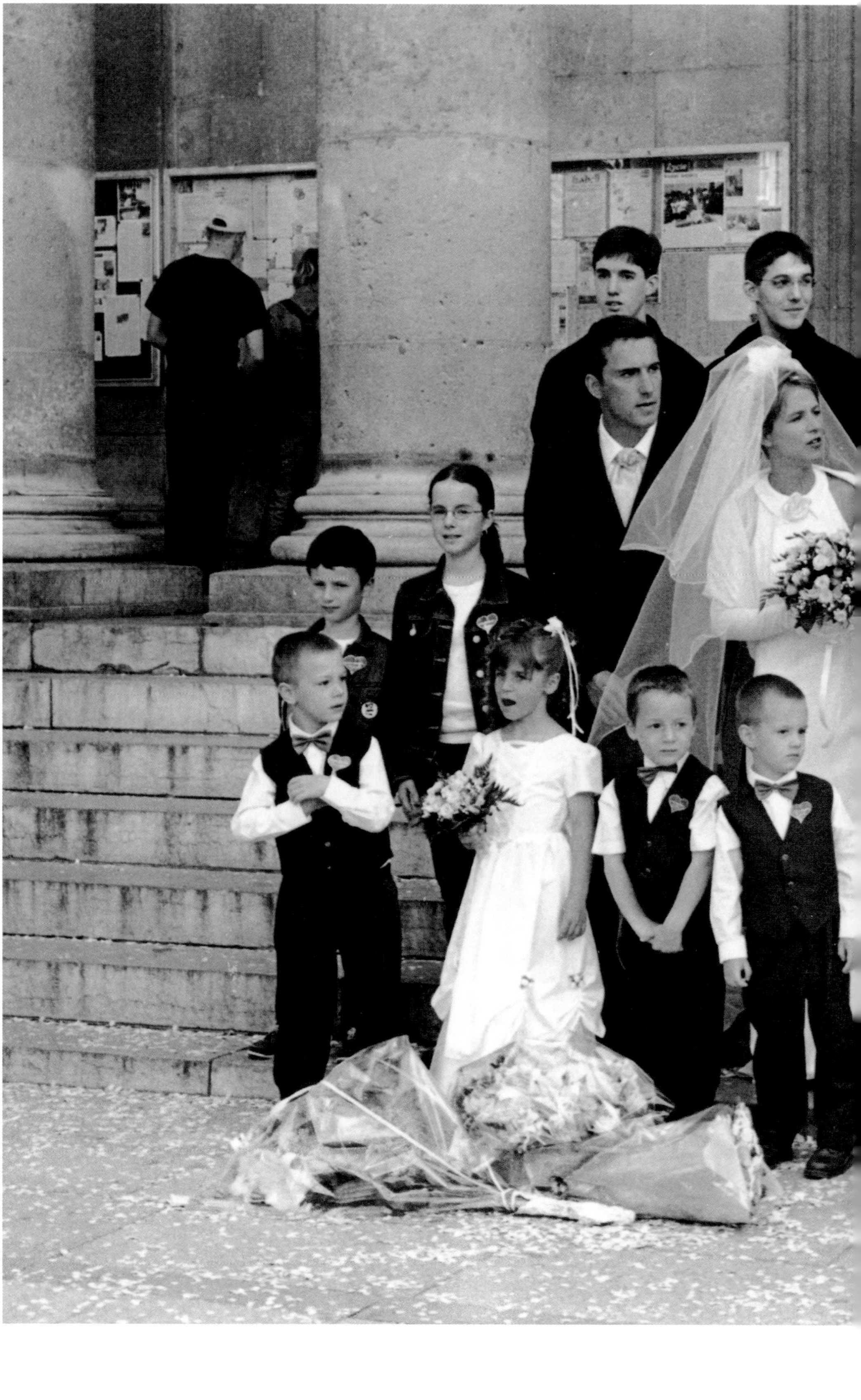

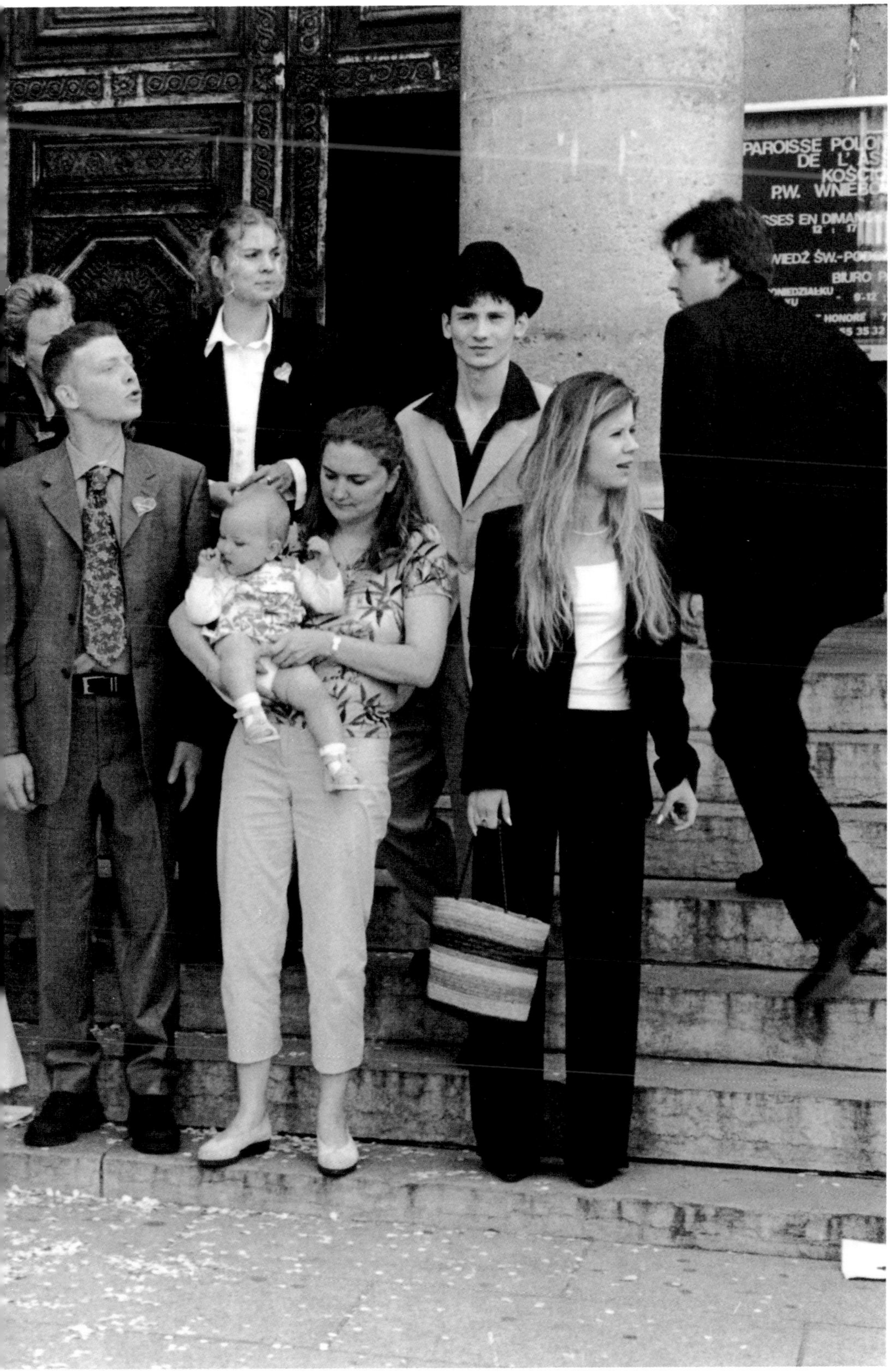

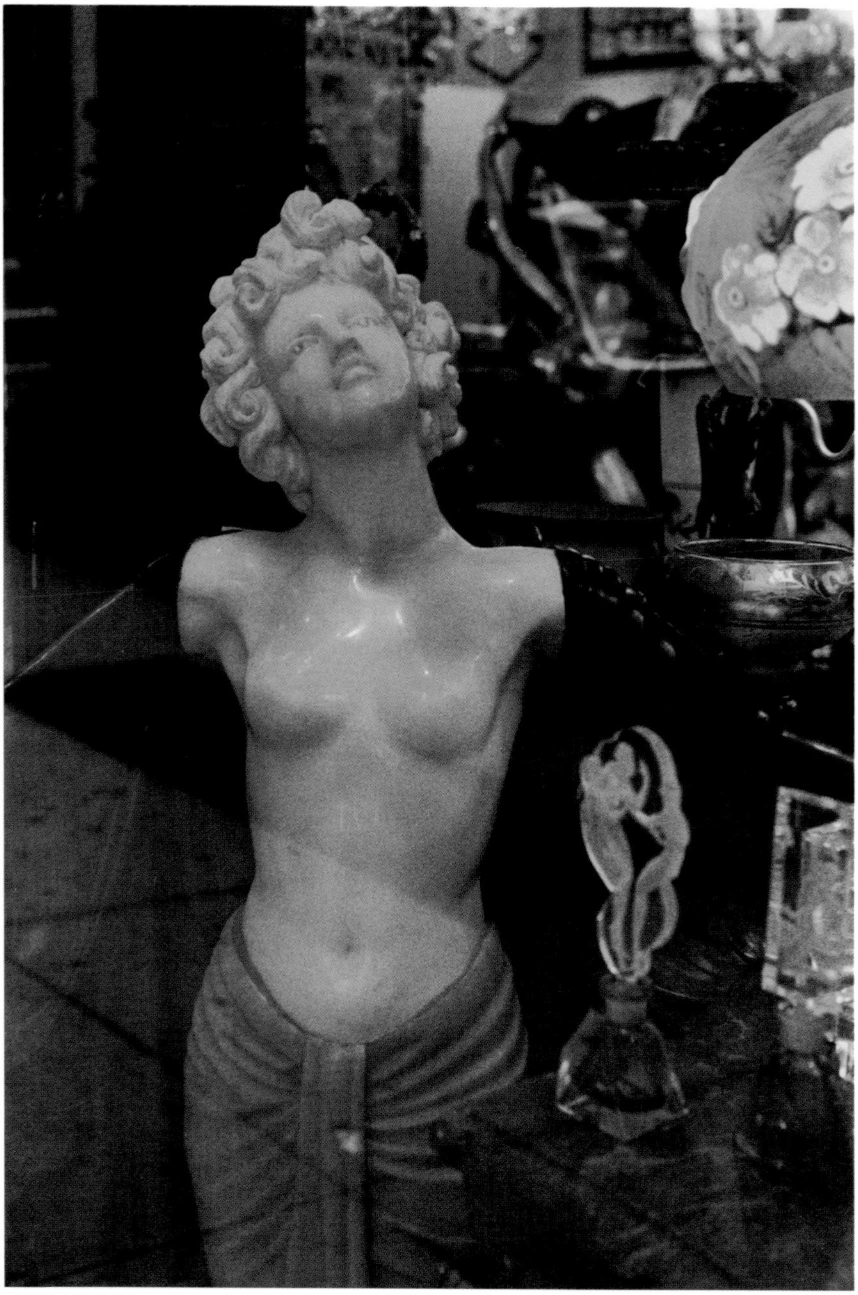

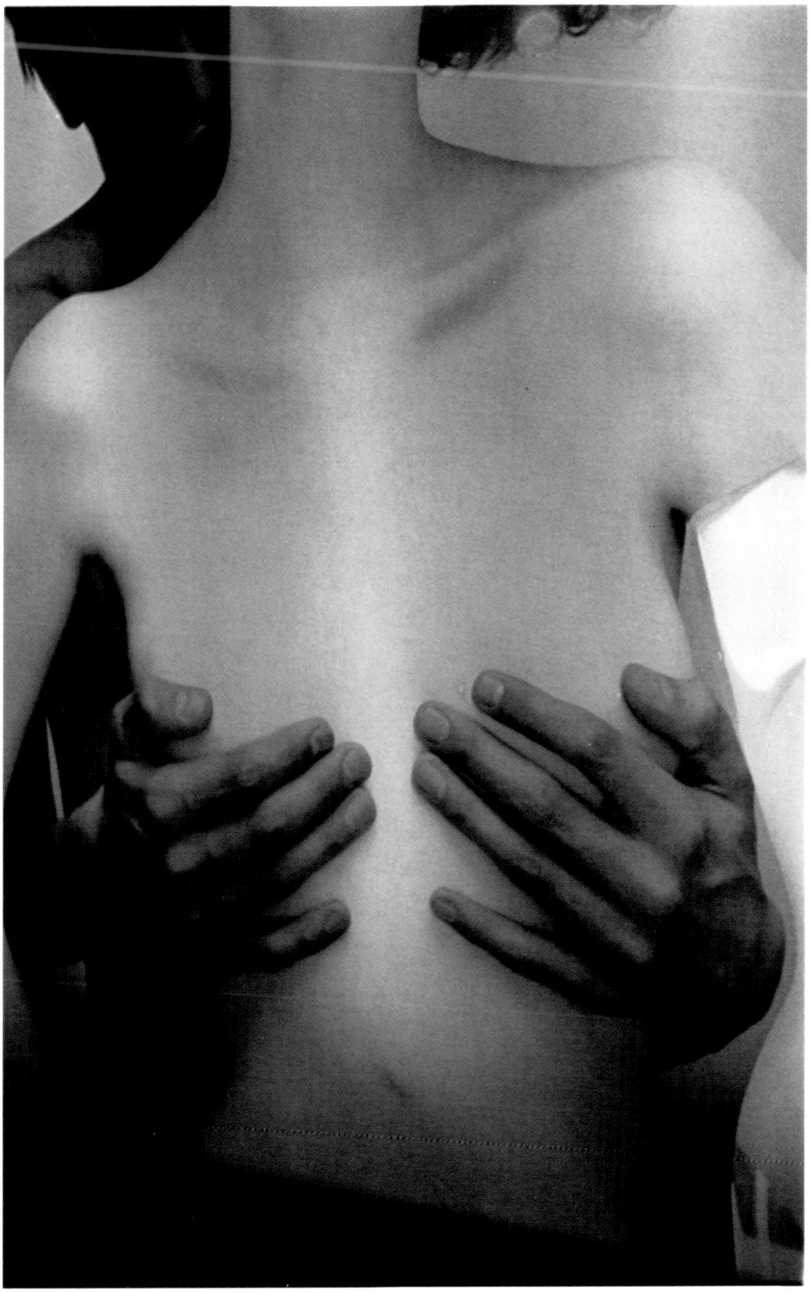

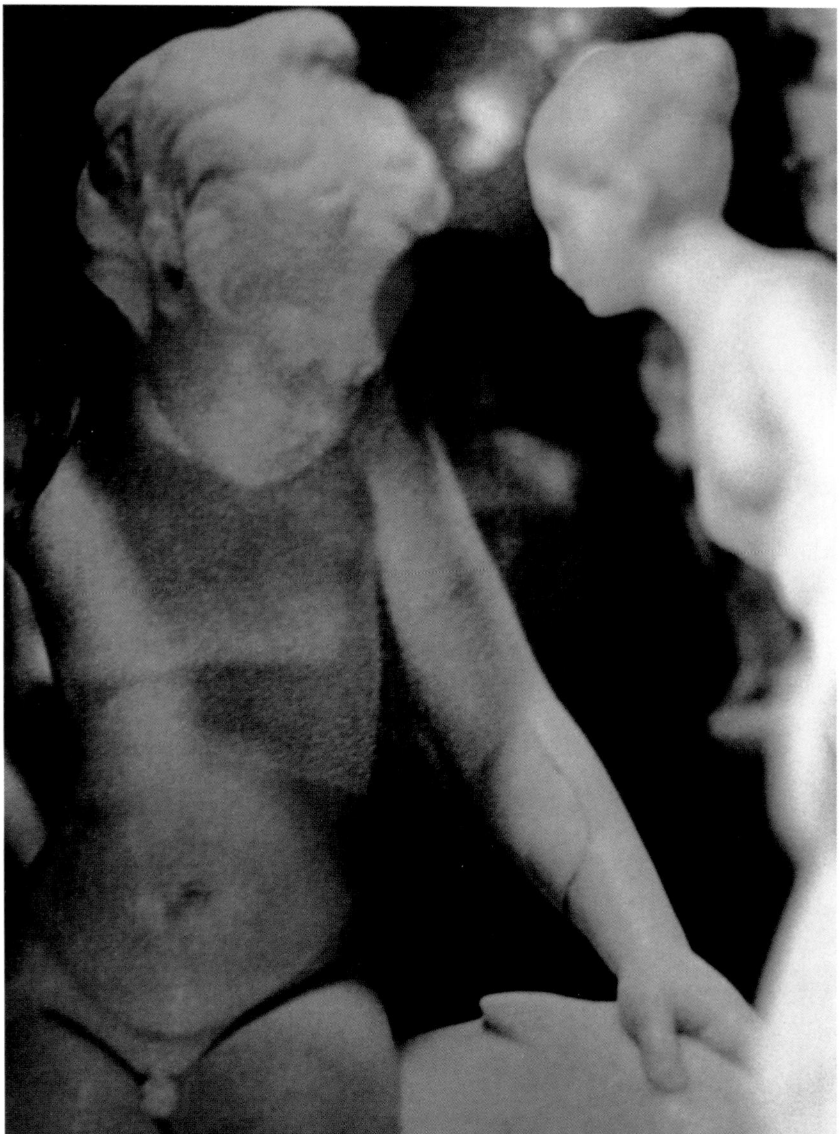

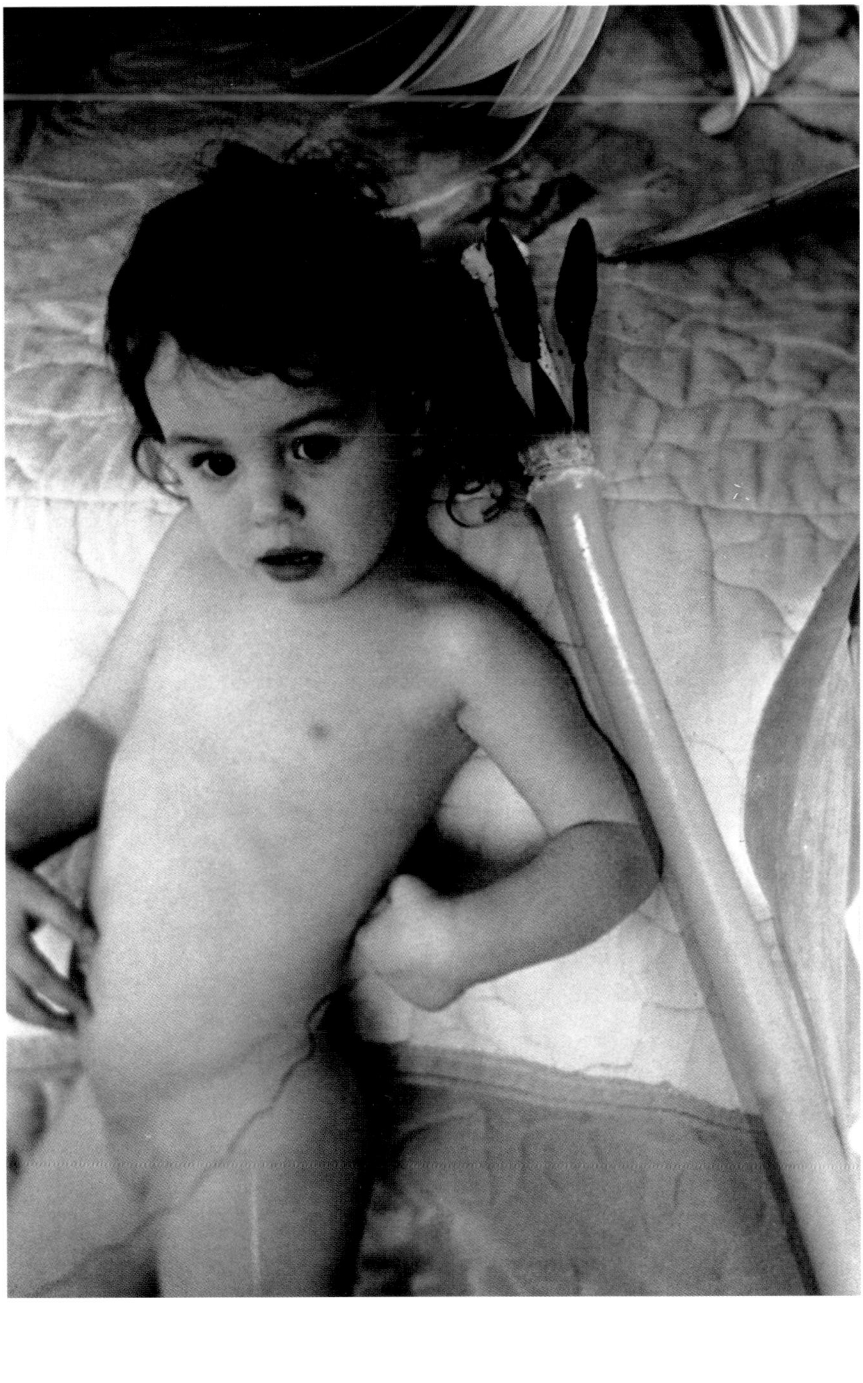

words unspoken at life's end

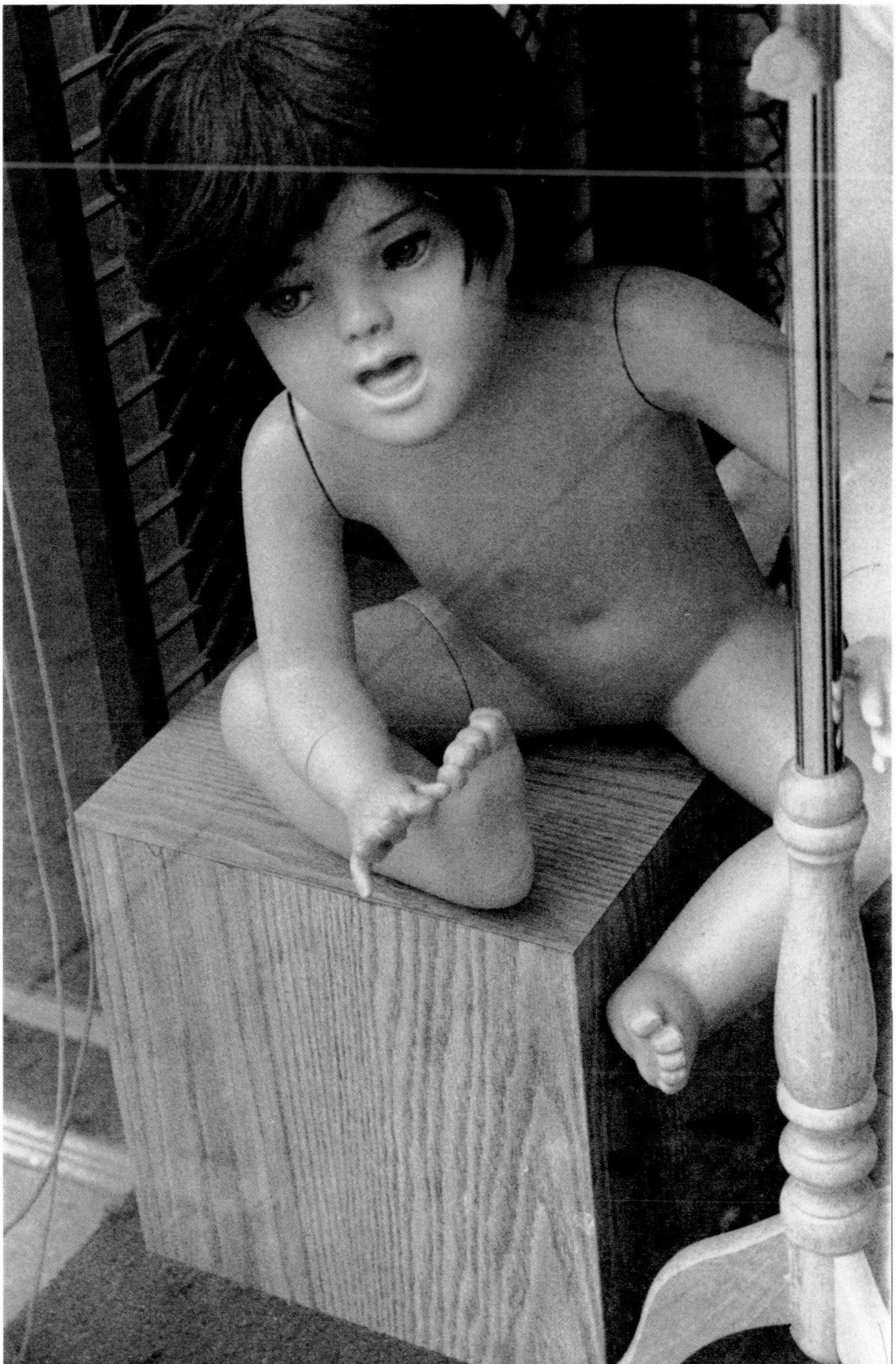

never wanting to say good-bye

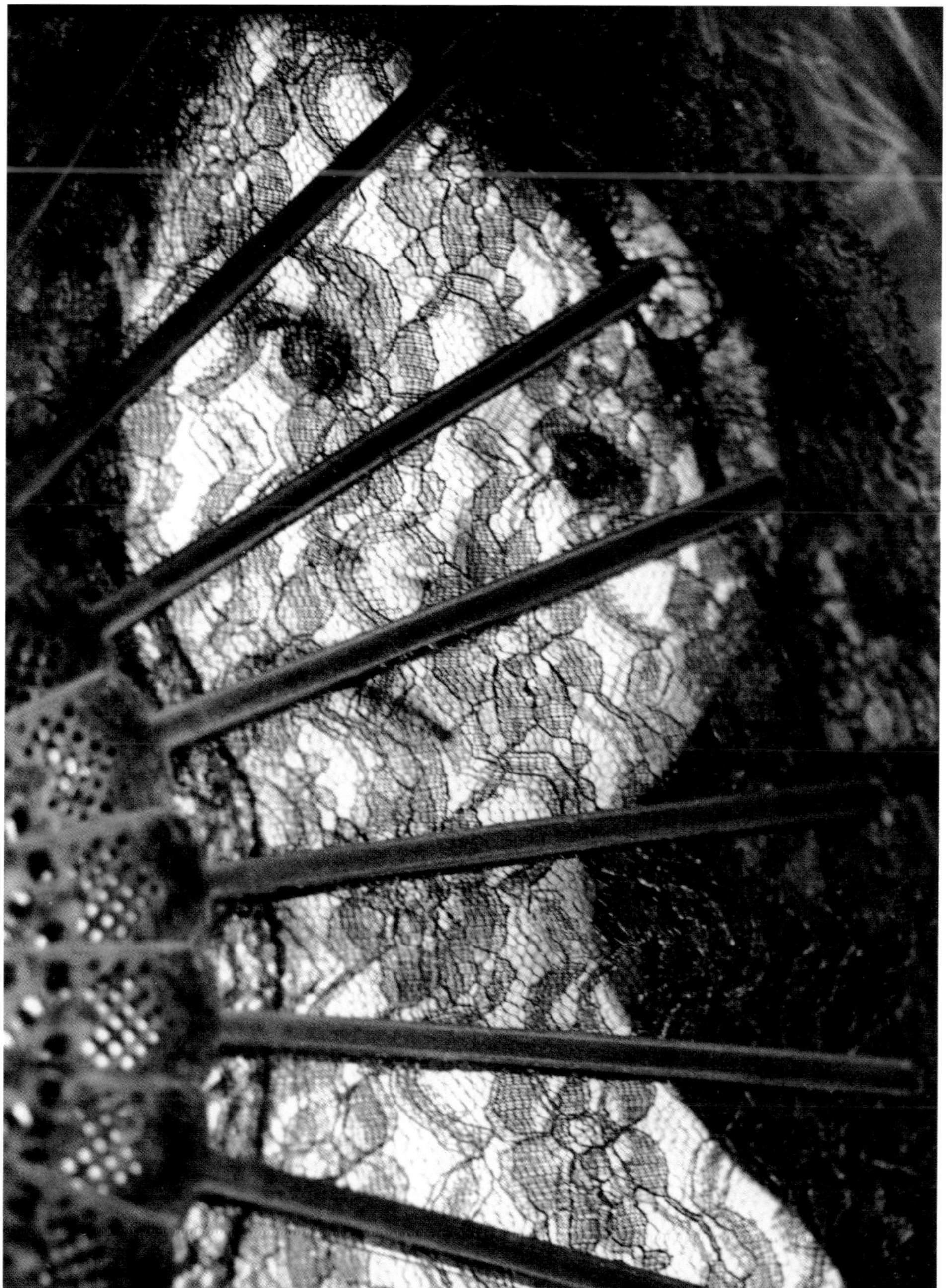

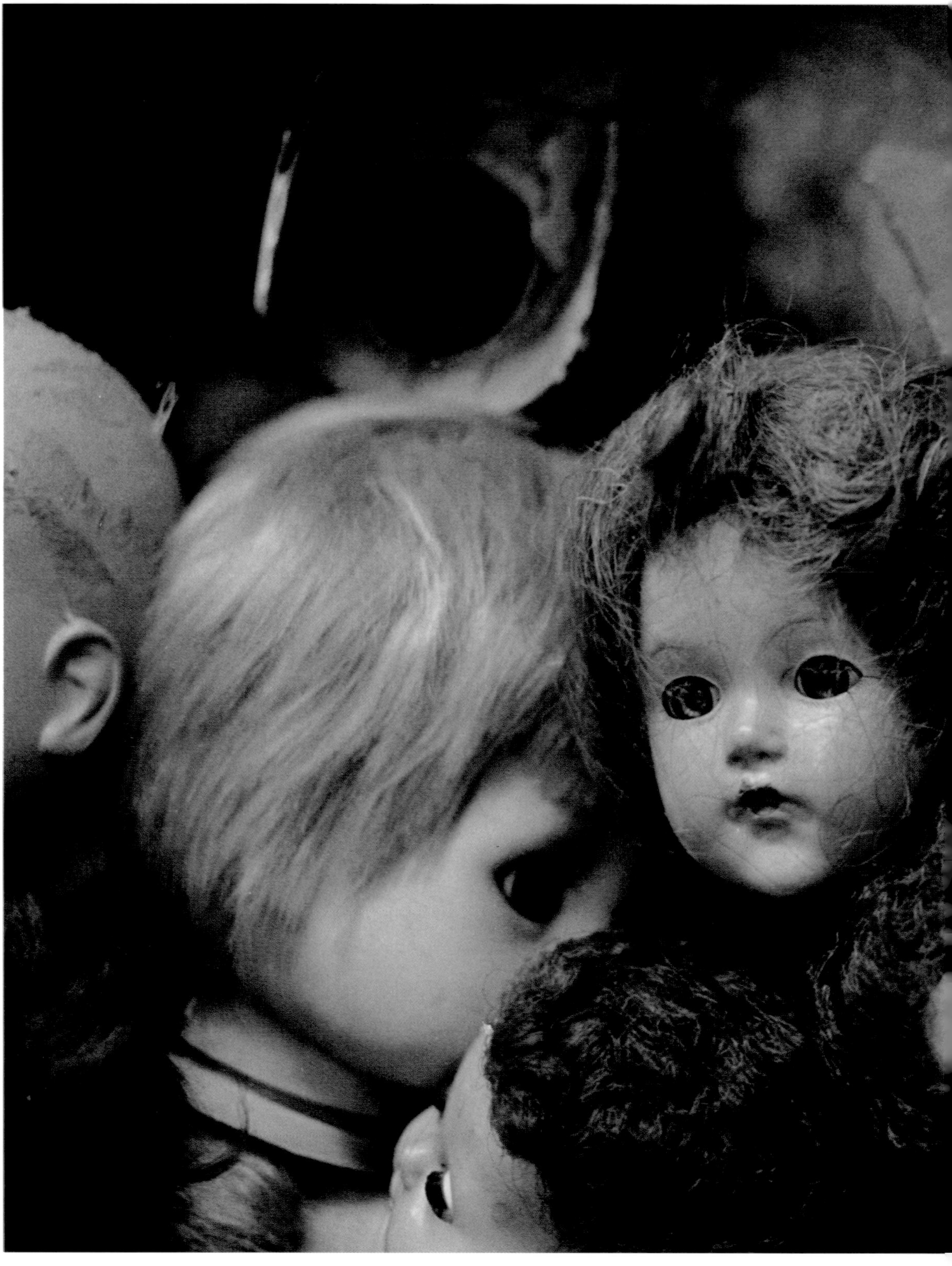

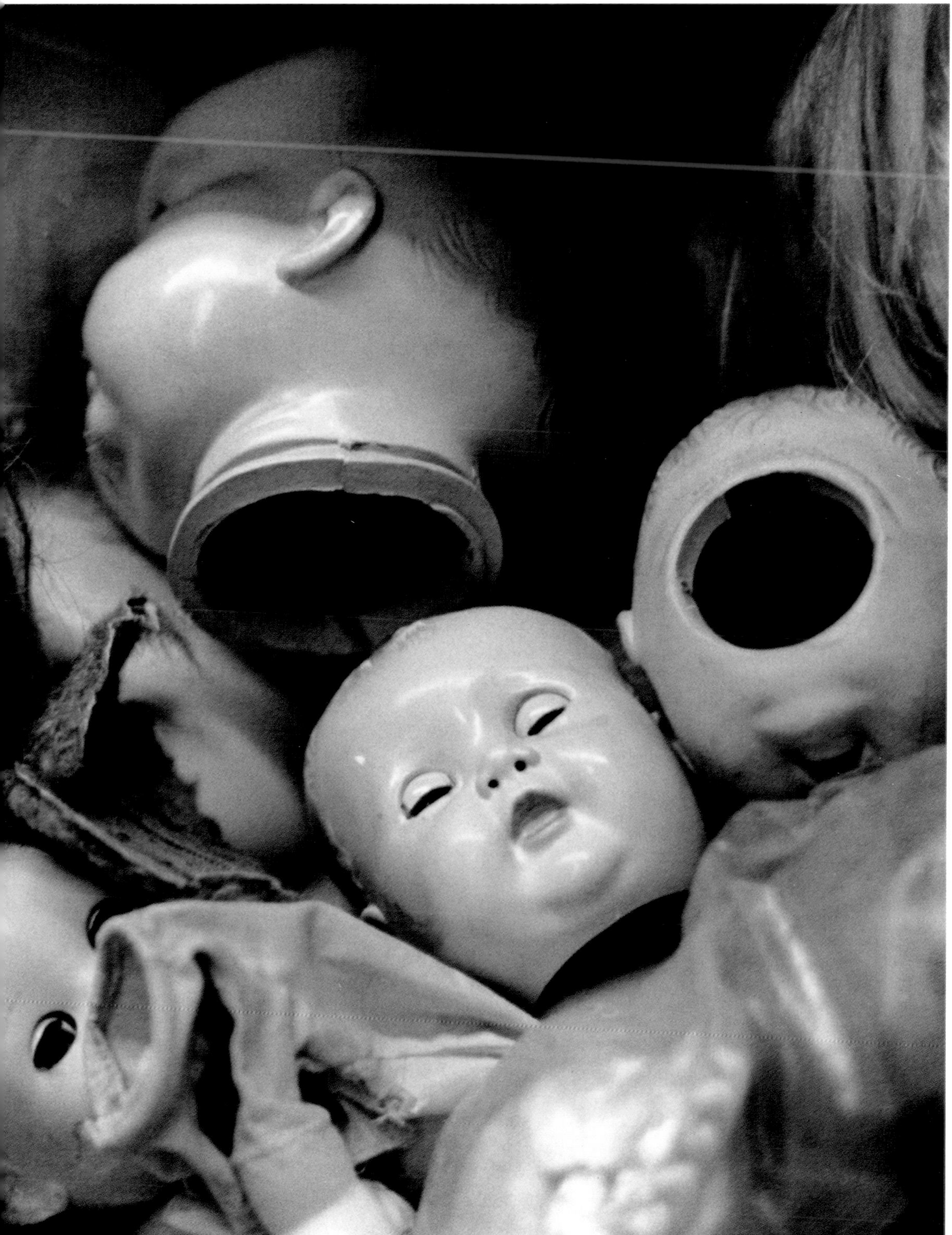

we wonder at the mystery surrounding our lives

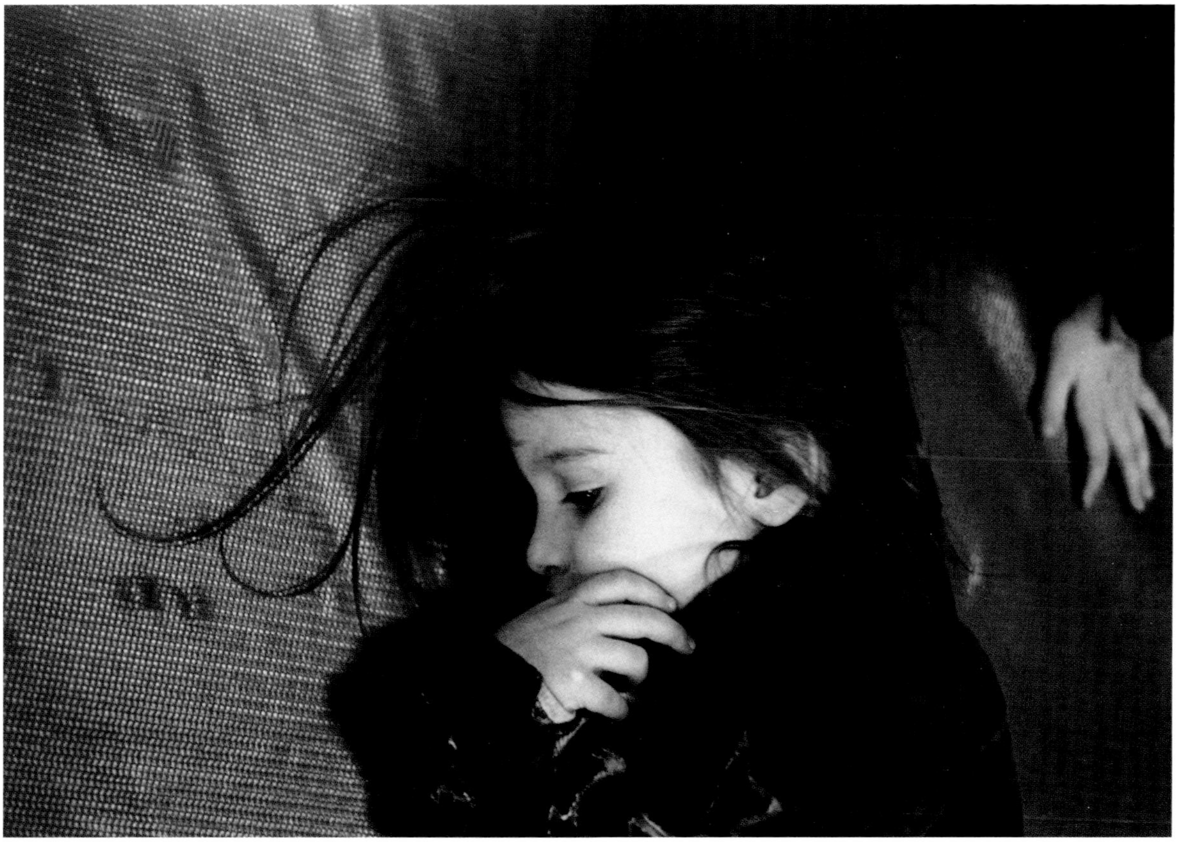

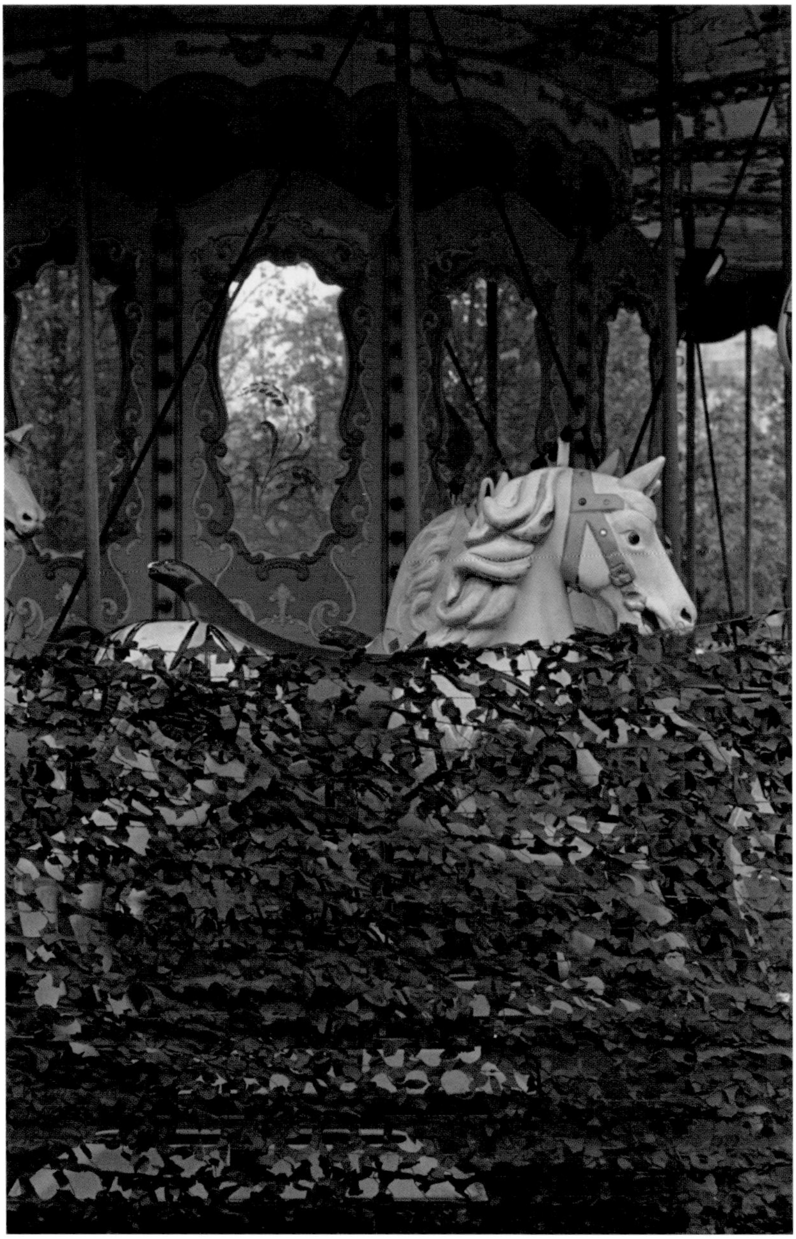

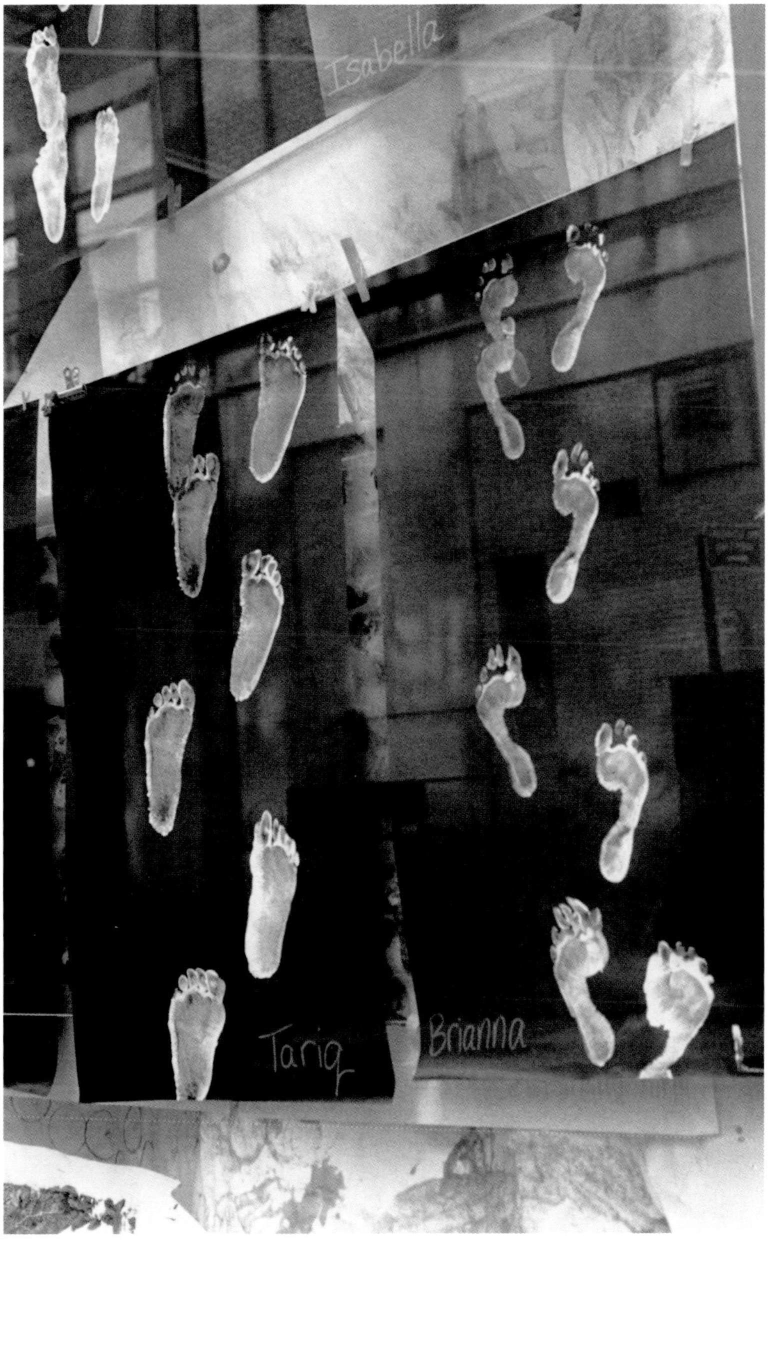
Isabella
Tariq
Brianna

to our sense of pity, beauty and pain,

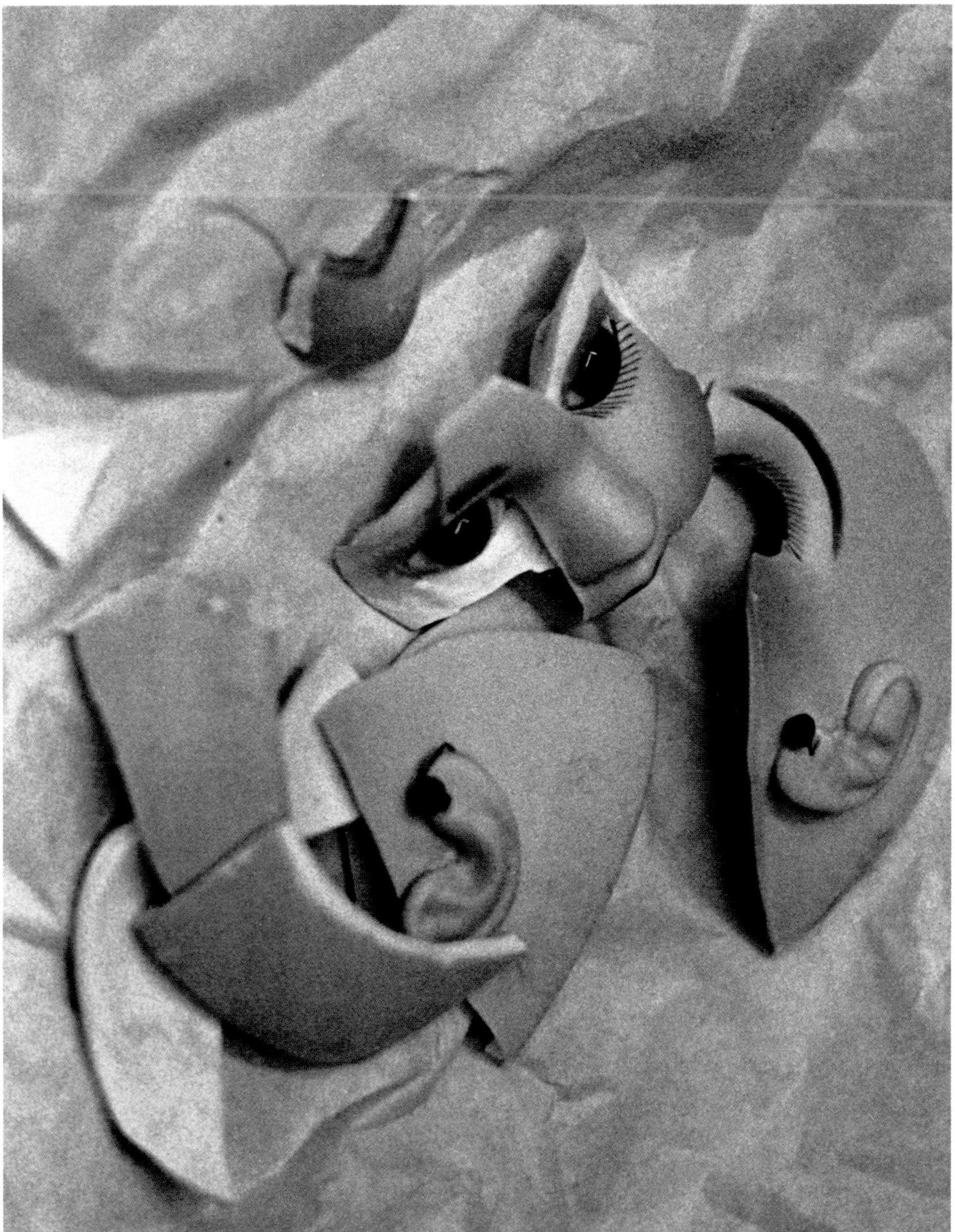

the latent feeling of fellowship with all creation...

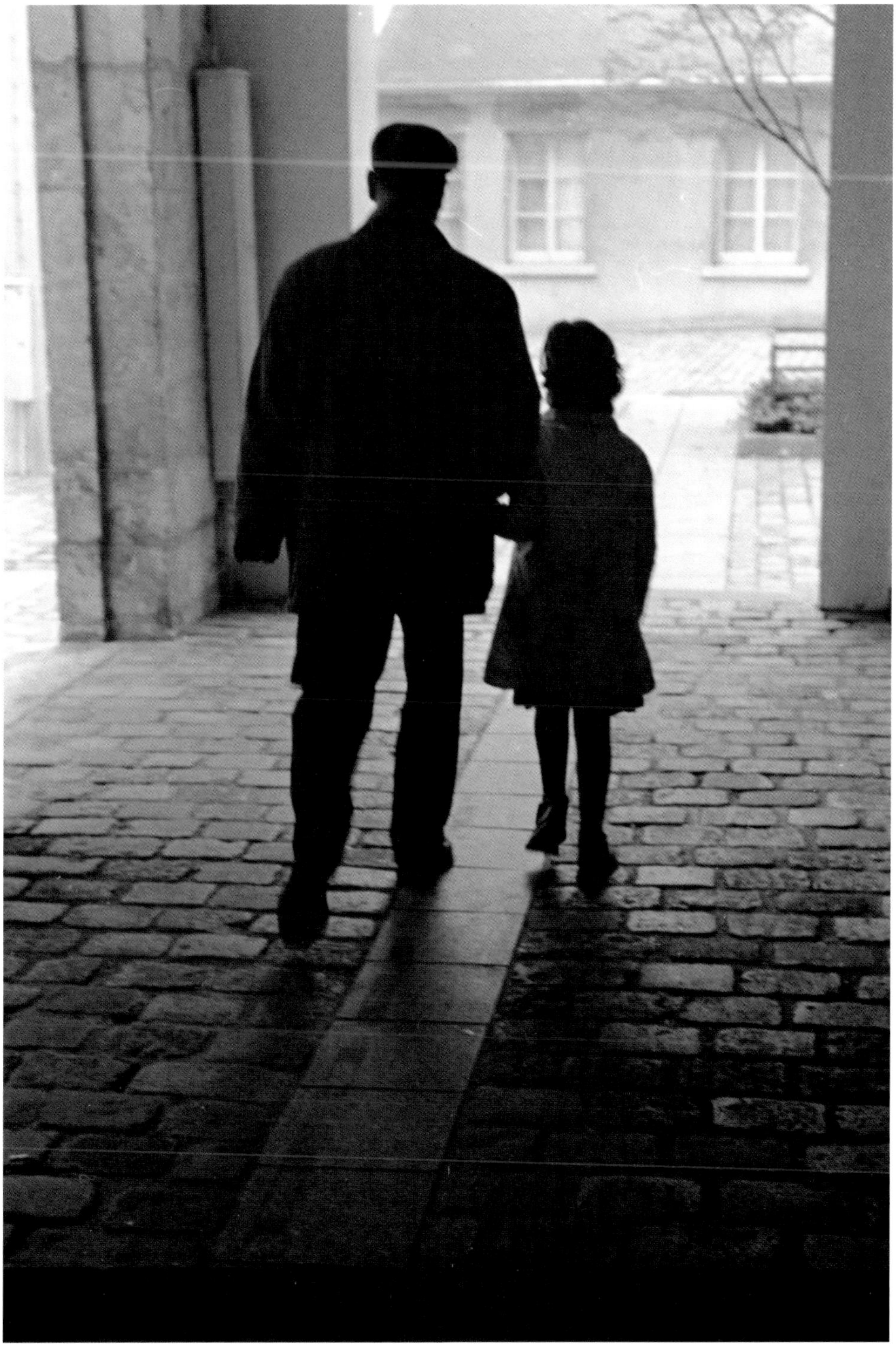

the loneliness of innumerable hearts
to the solidarity in dreams, in joy,

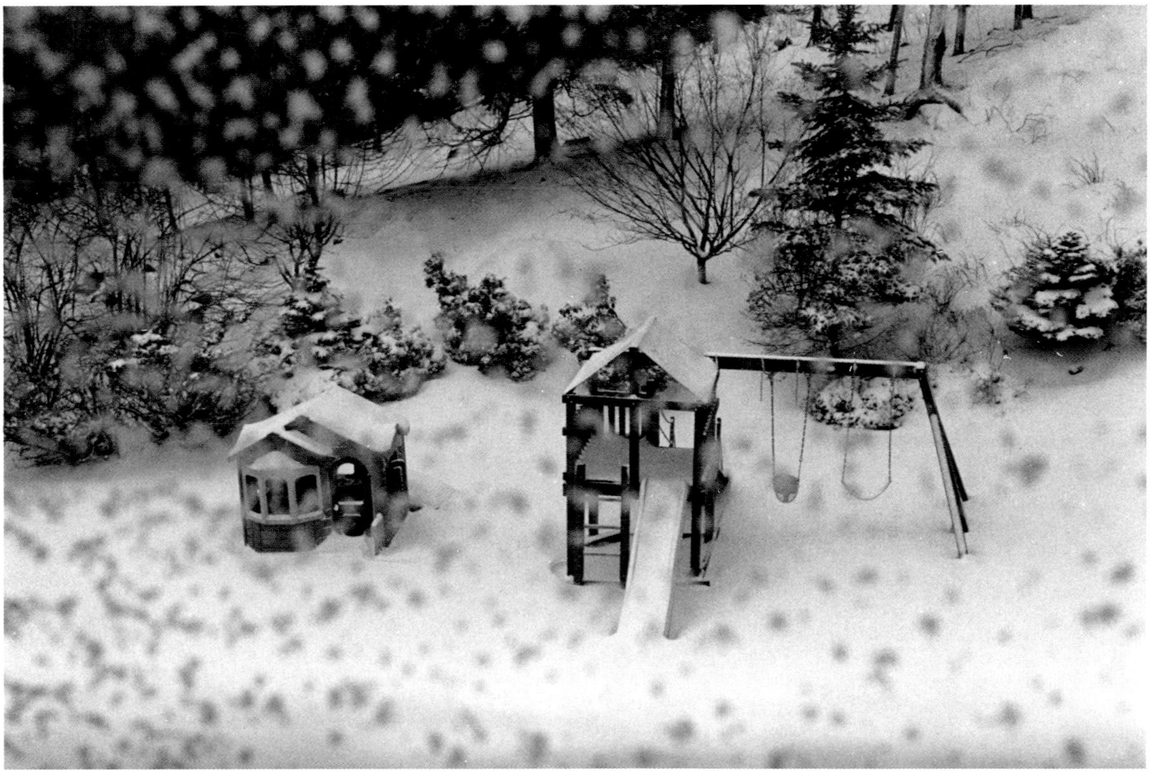

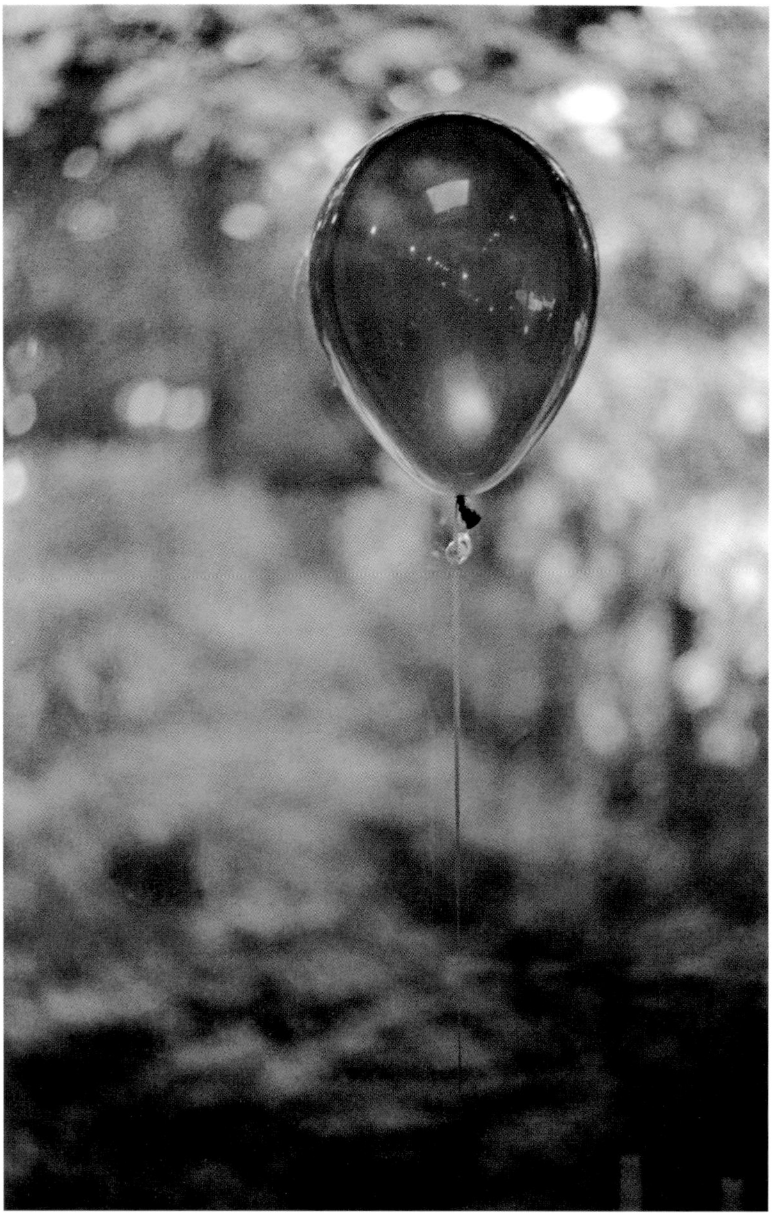

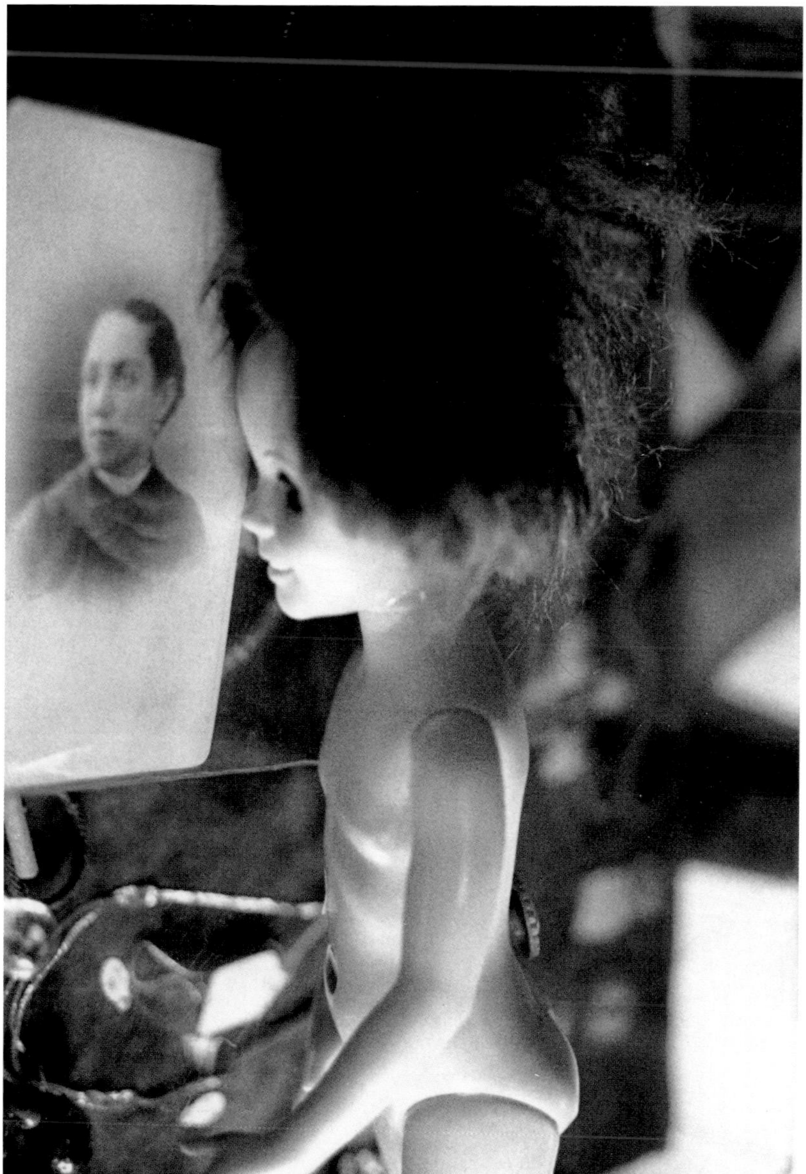

in sorrow, in aspirations

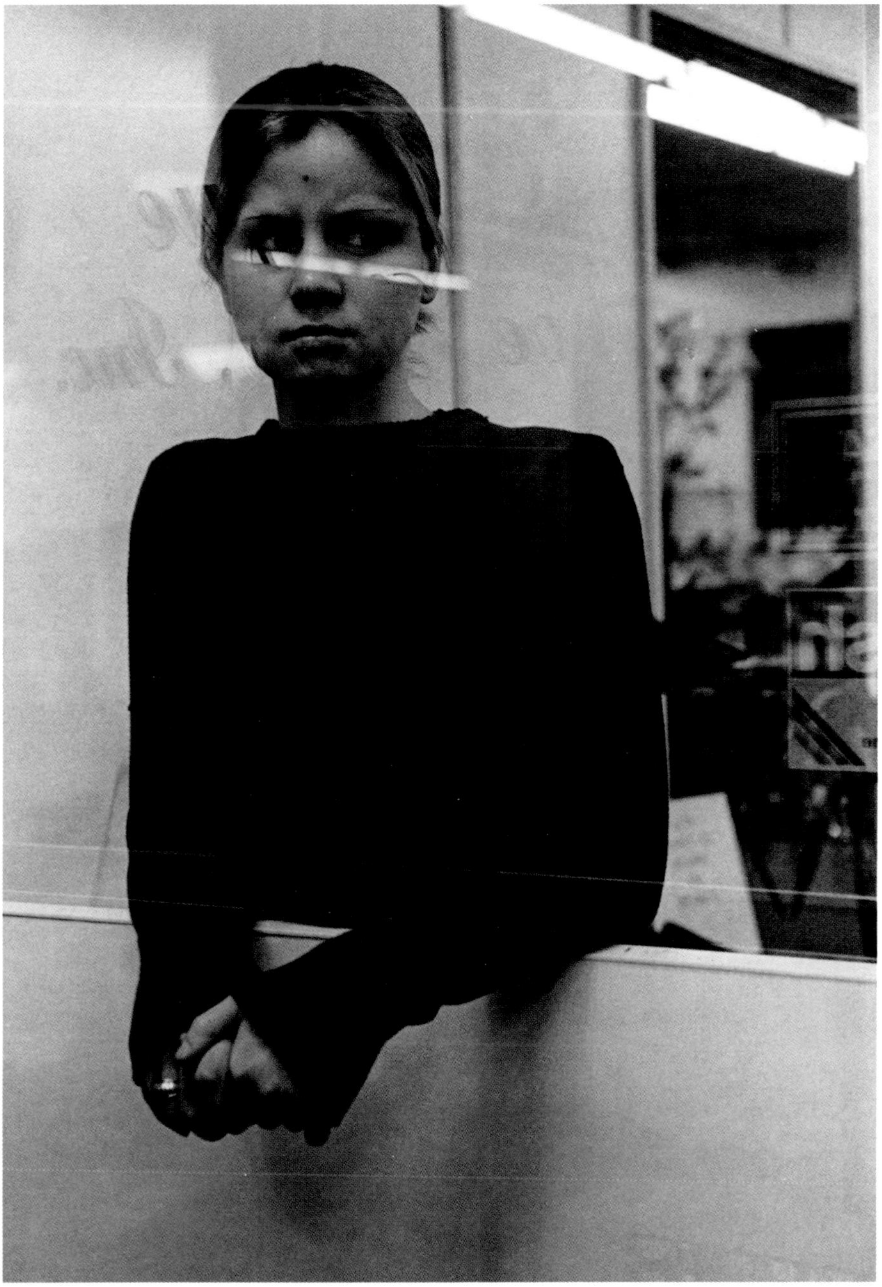

in illusions, in hope,

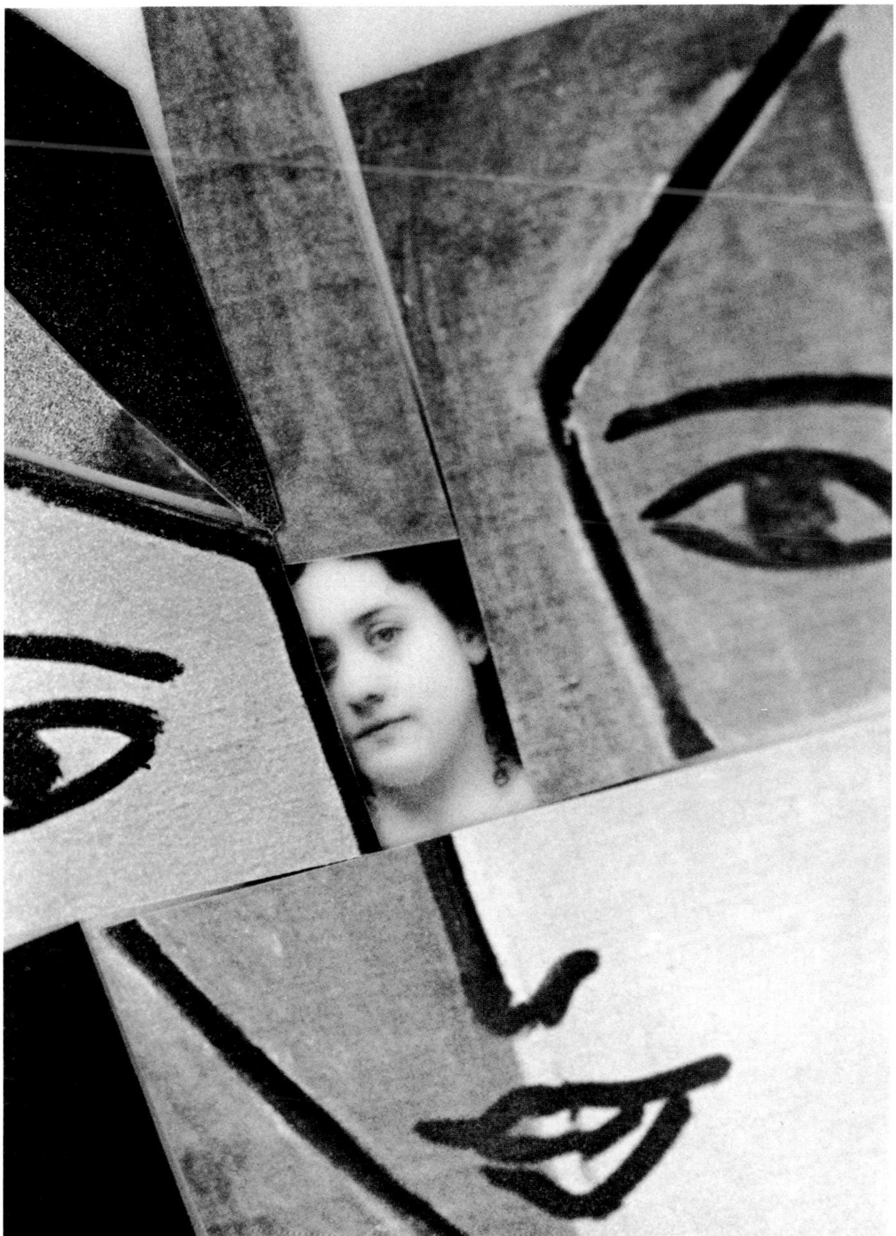

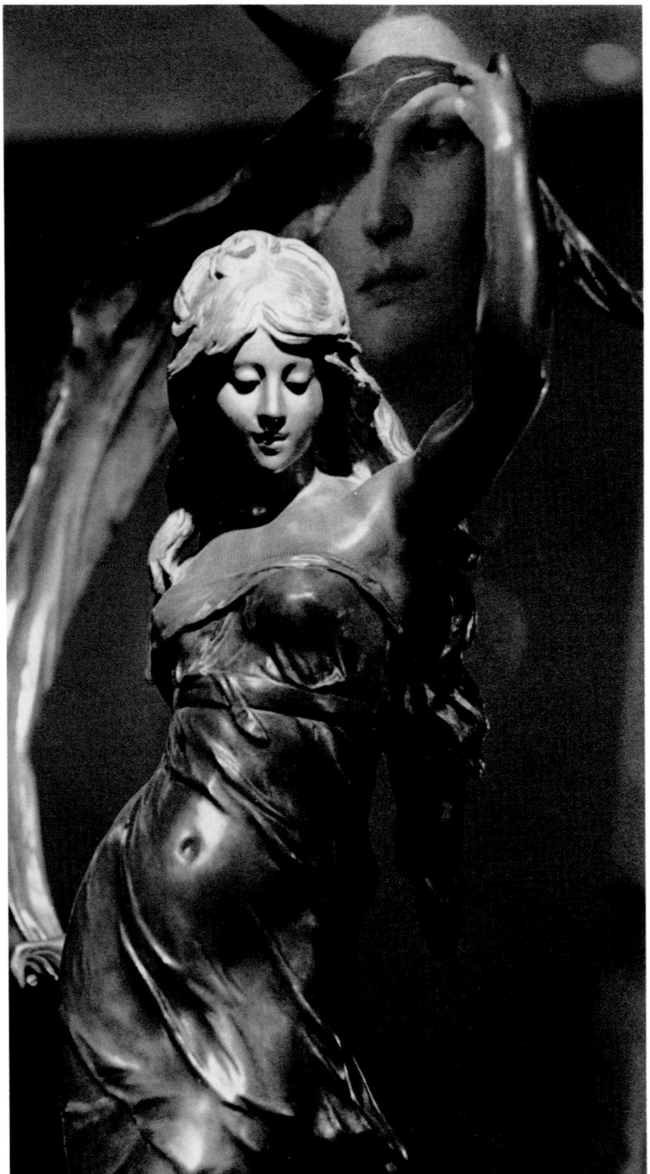

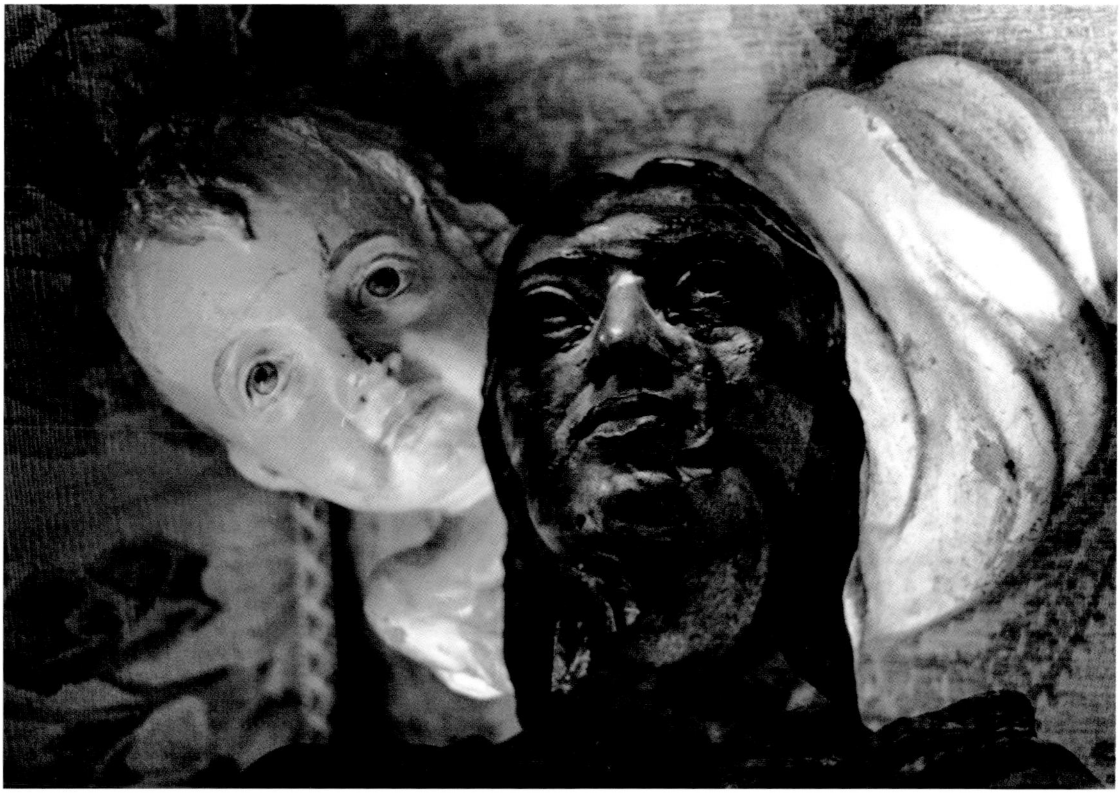

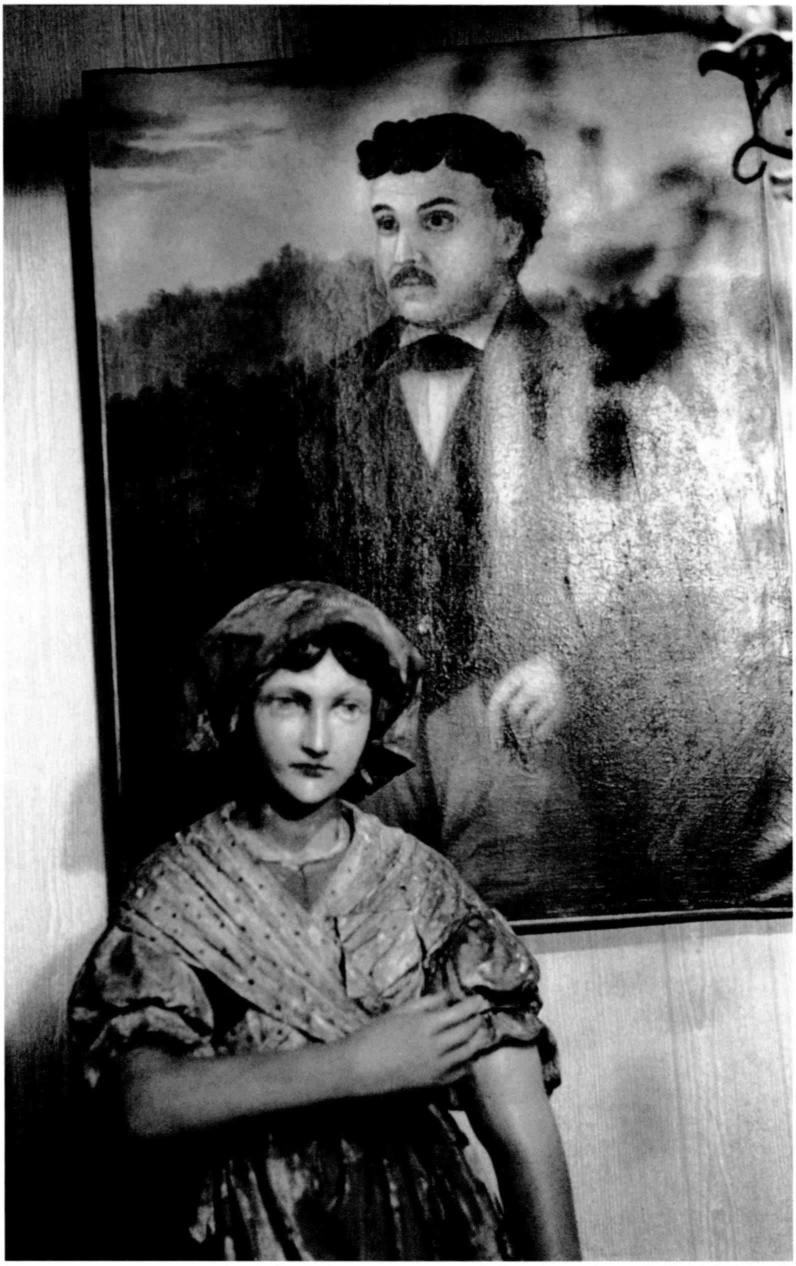

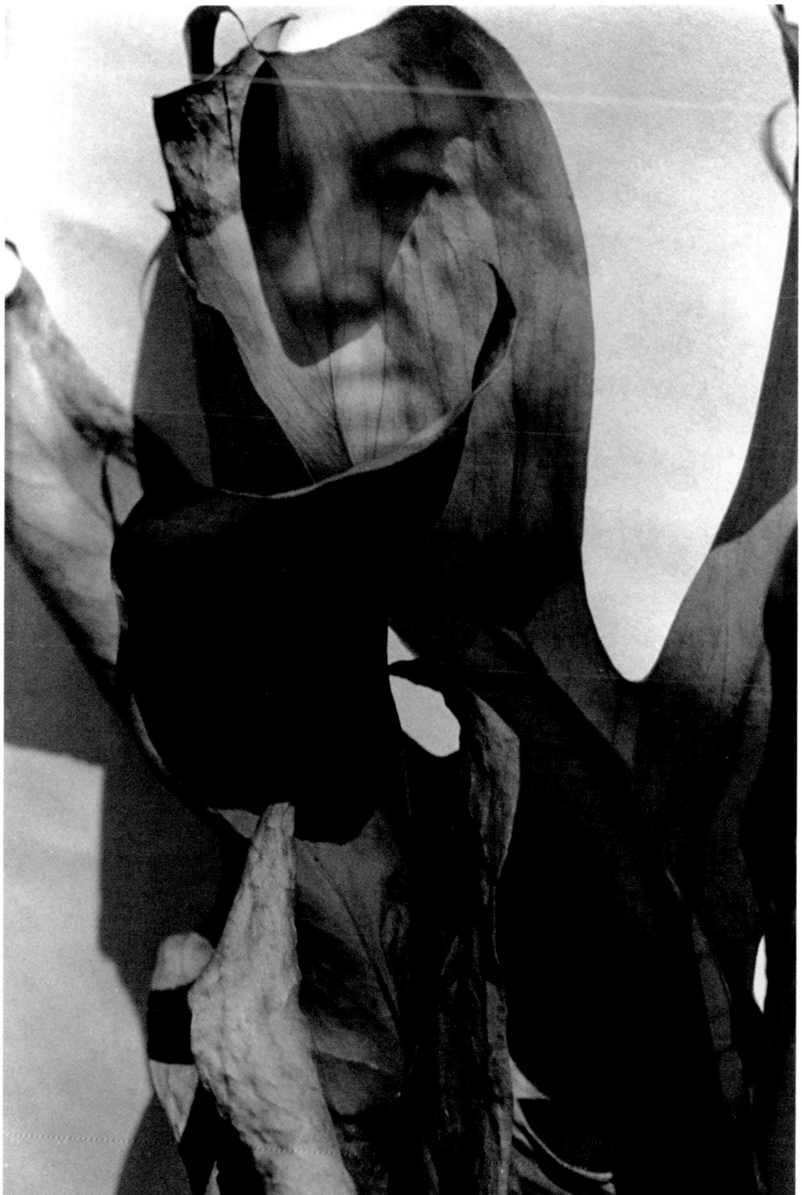

in fear which binds men to each other,

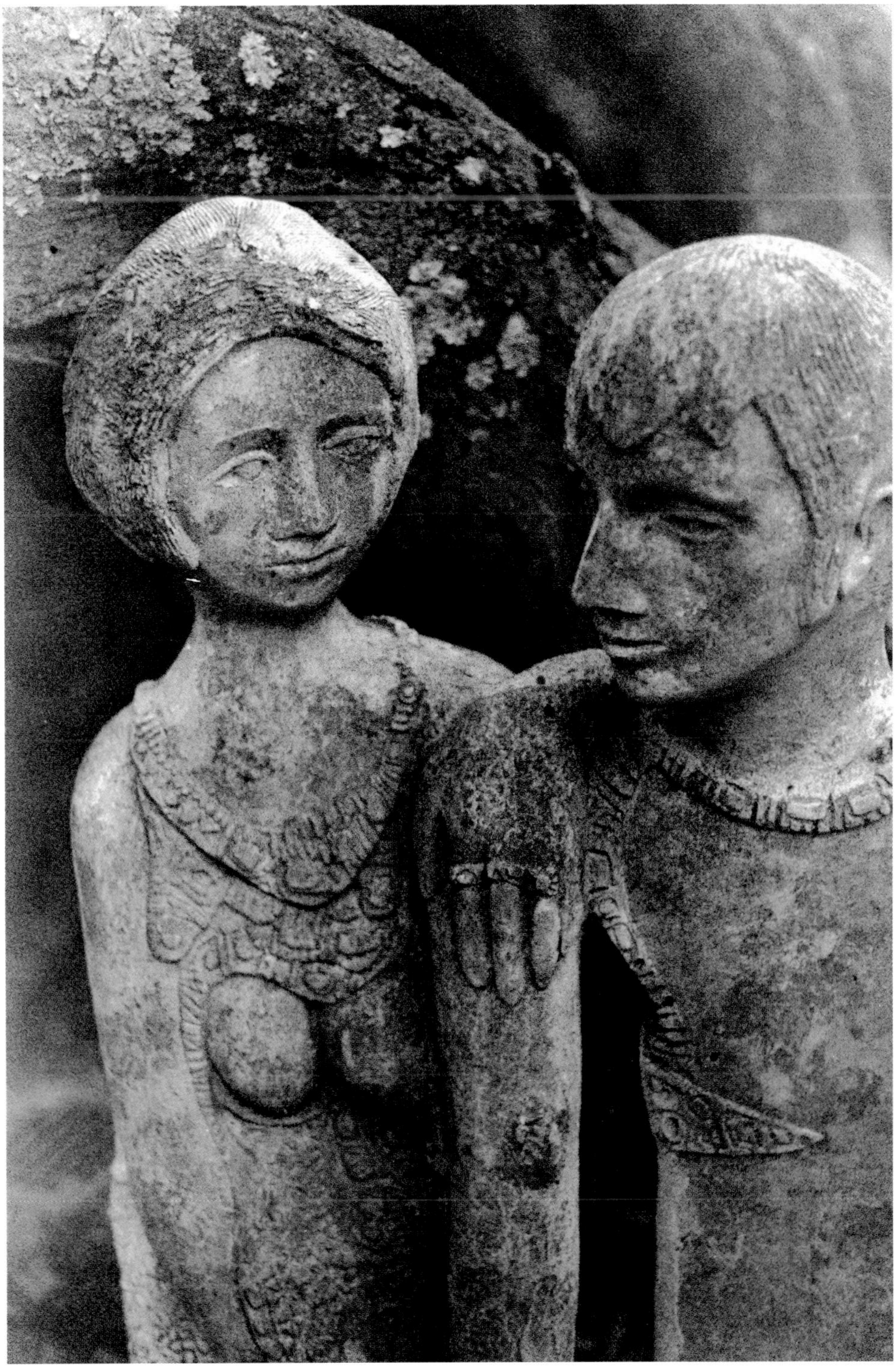

which binds together all humanity—

the dead to the living

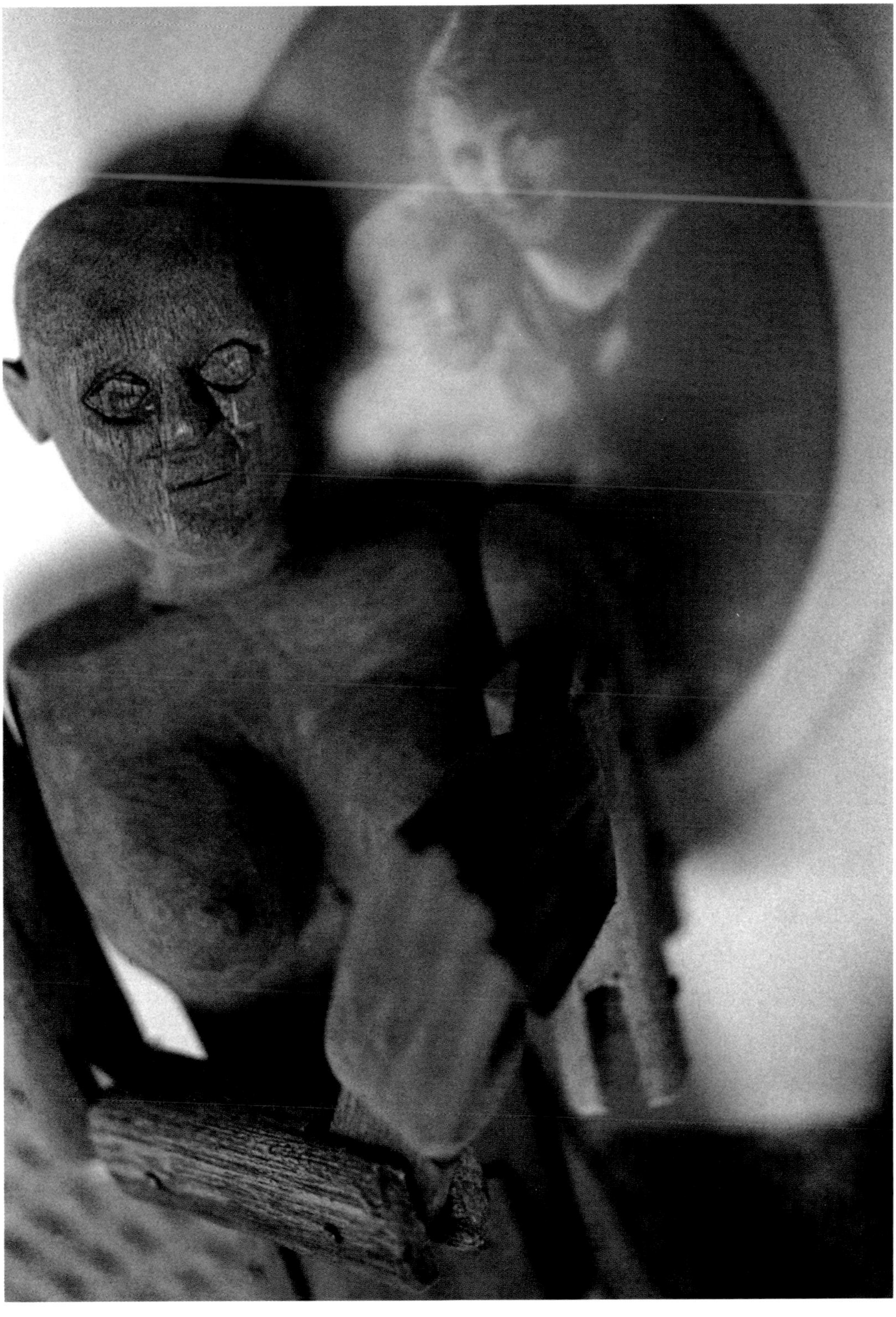

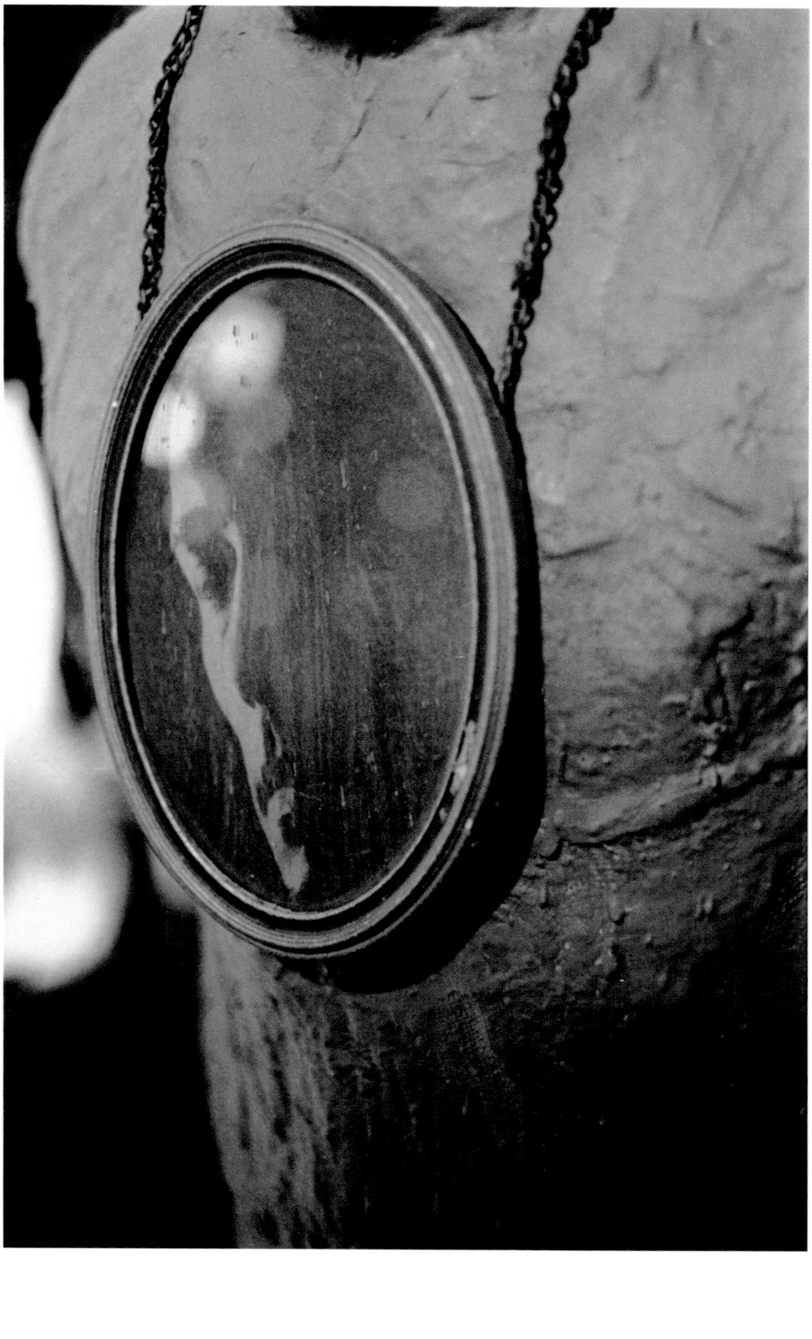

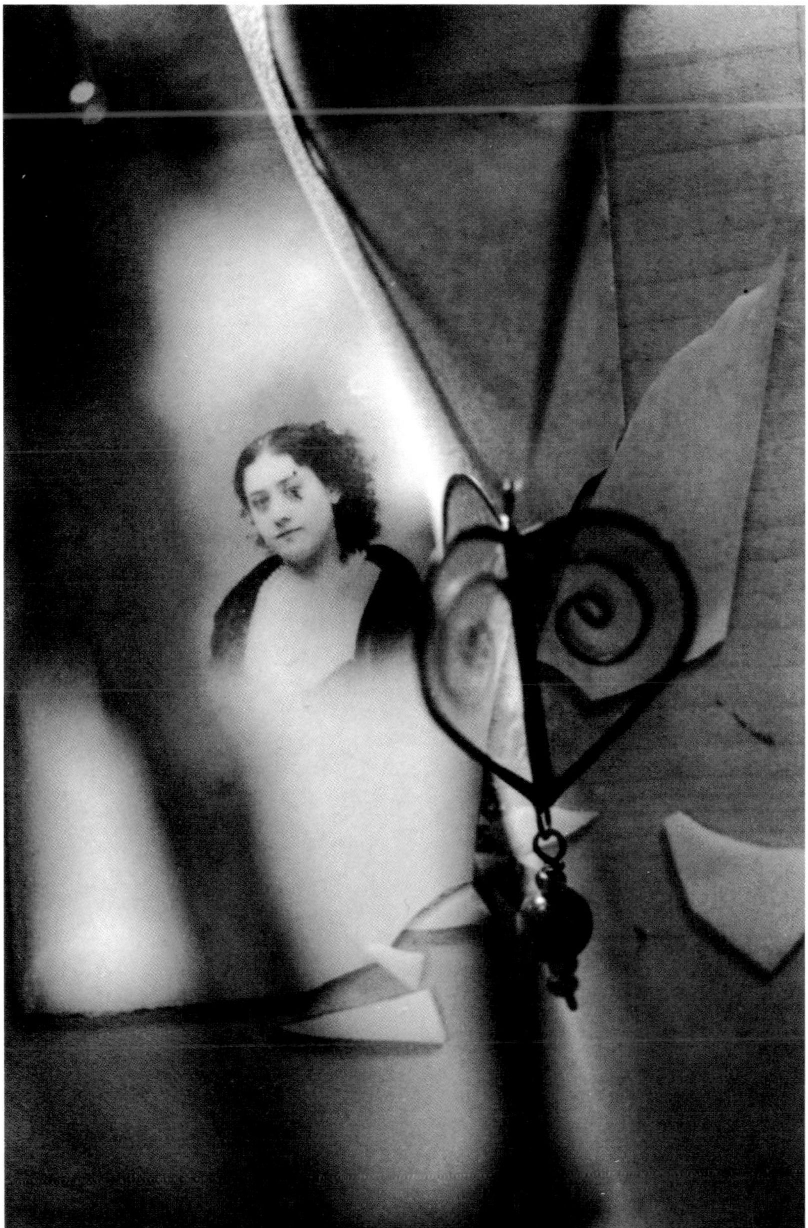

*and the living to the unborn.**

*Joseph Conrad, "The Nigger of Narcissus"

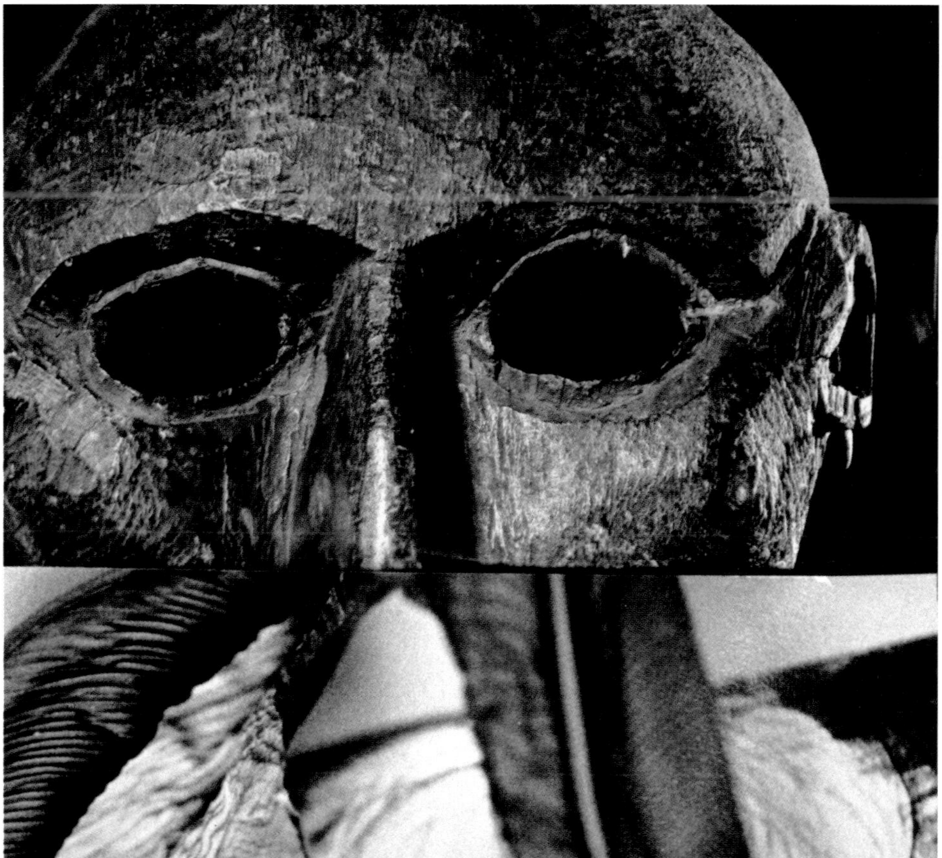

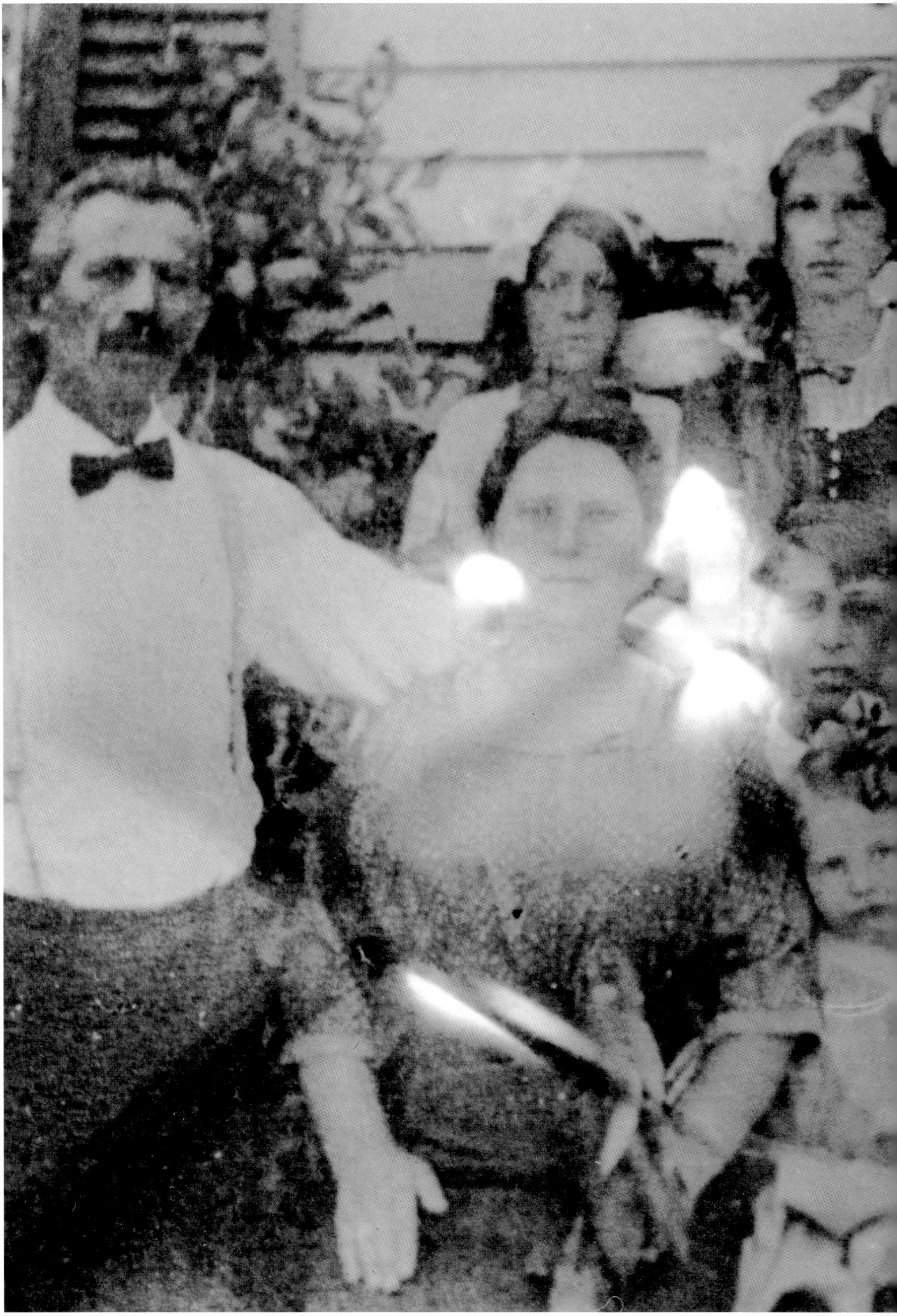

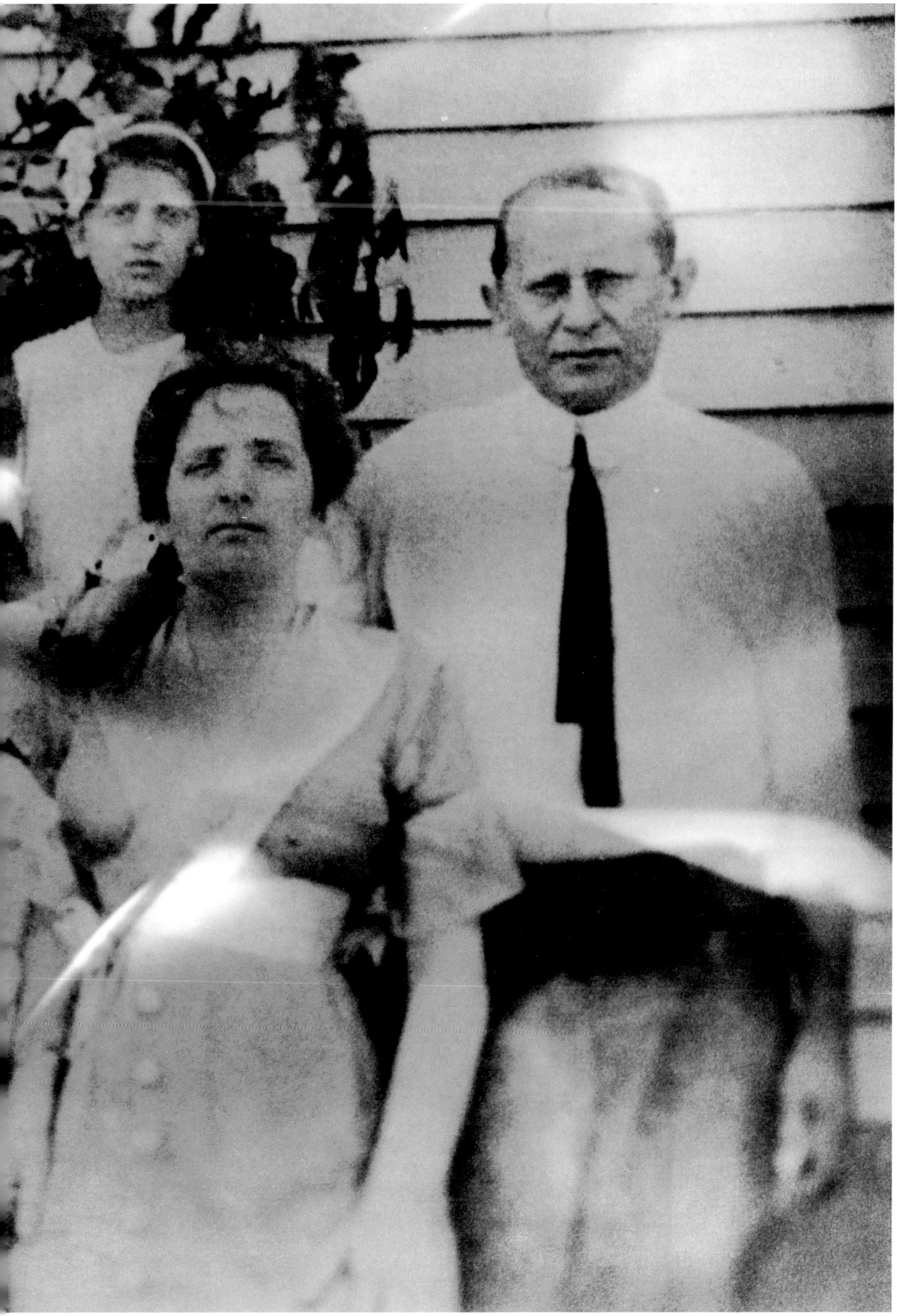

days are almost gone before they arrive

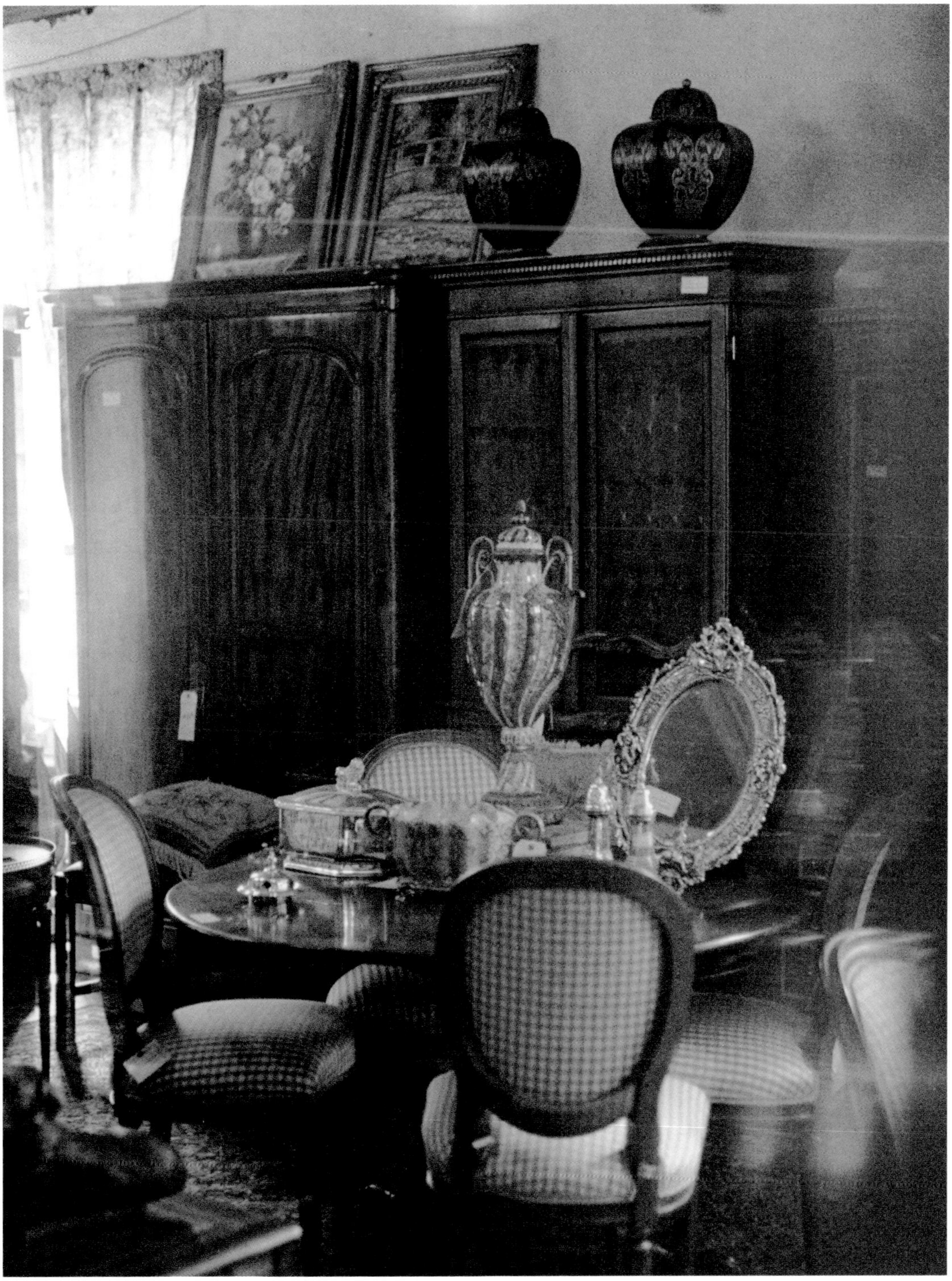

the moon gives light to my shadow,
the mirror of myself I see

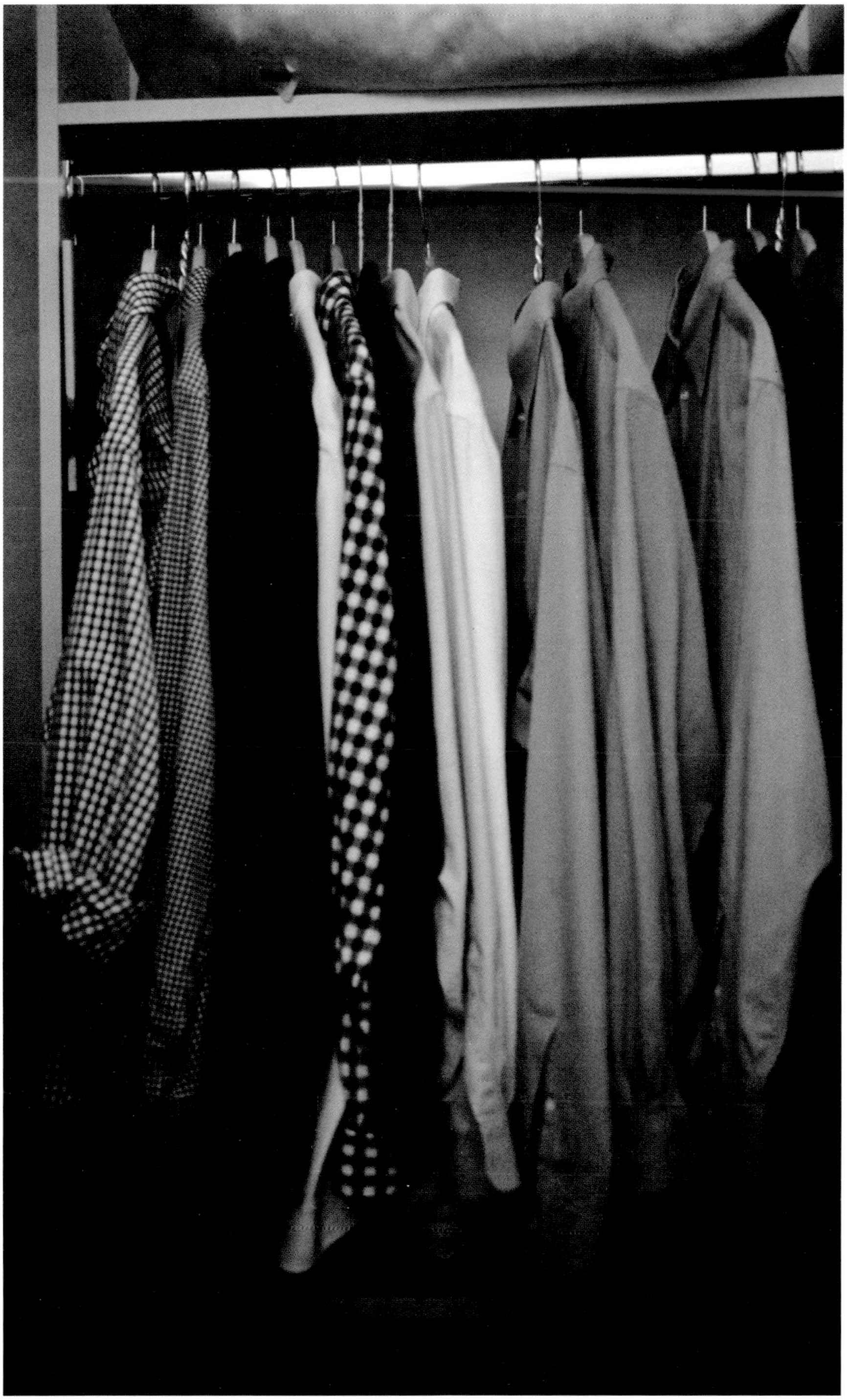

watching you

watching me.

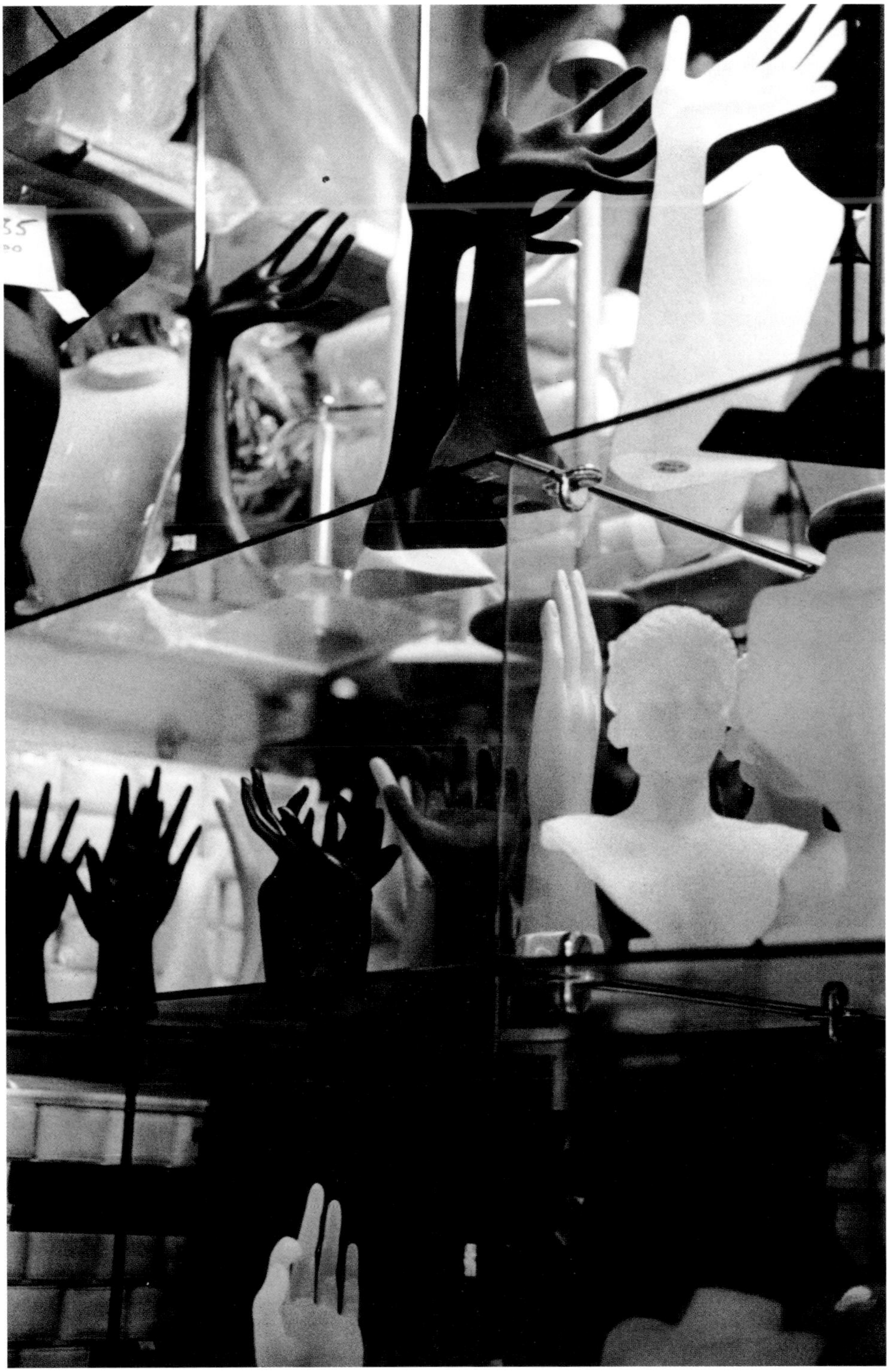

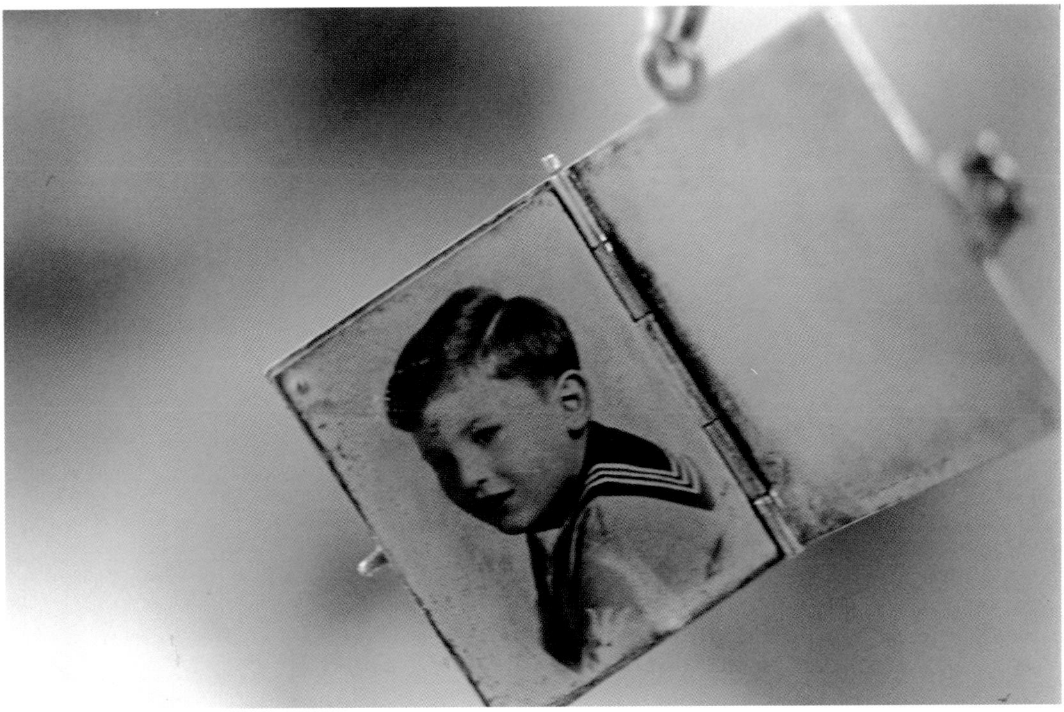

your eyes are mine

disappearing reflections

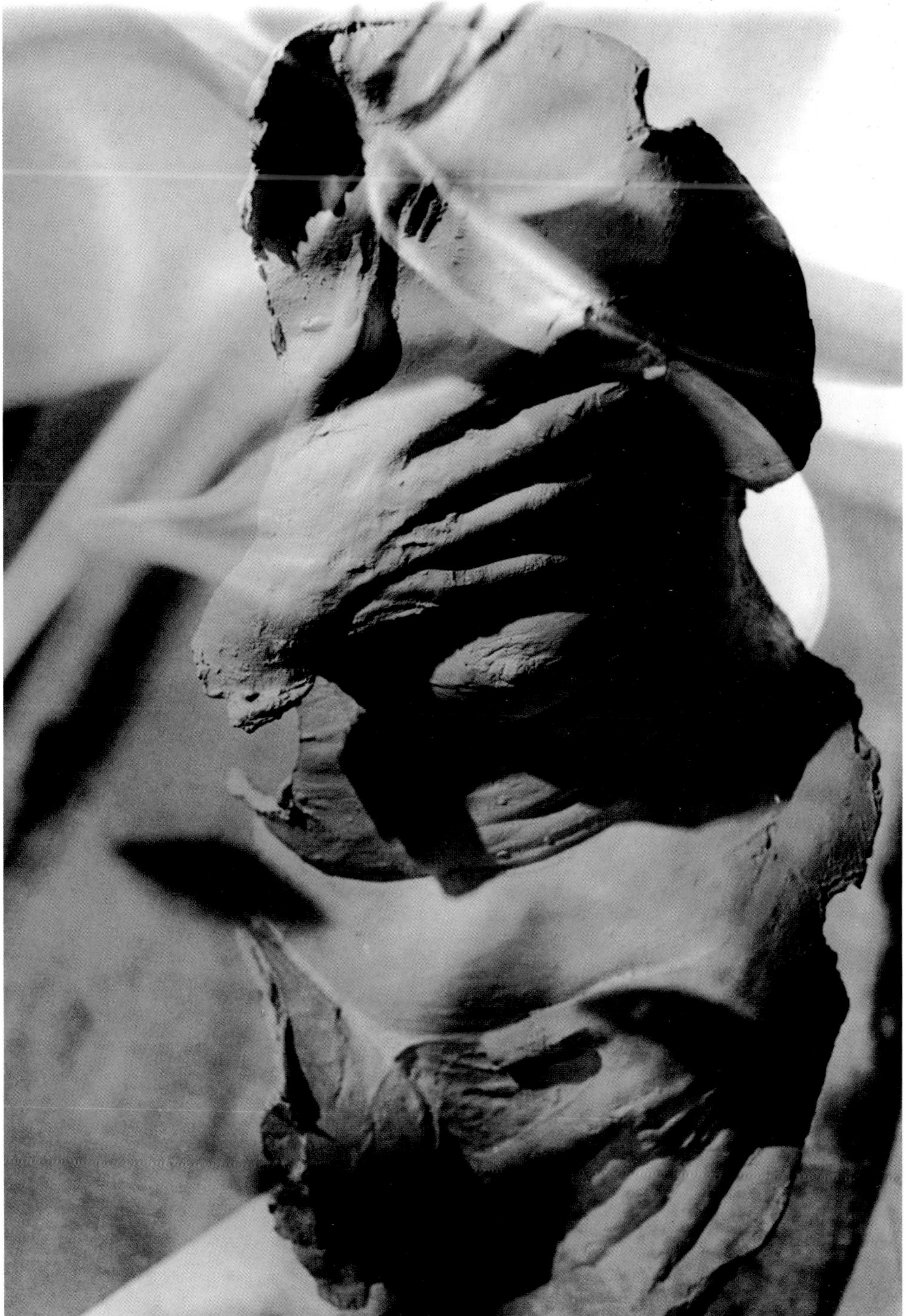

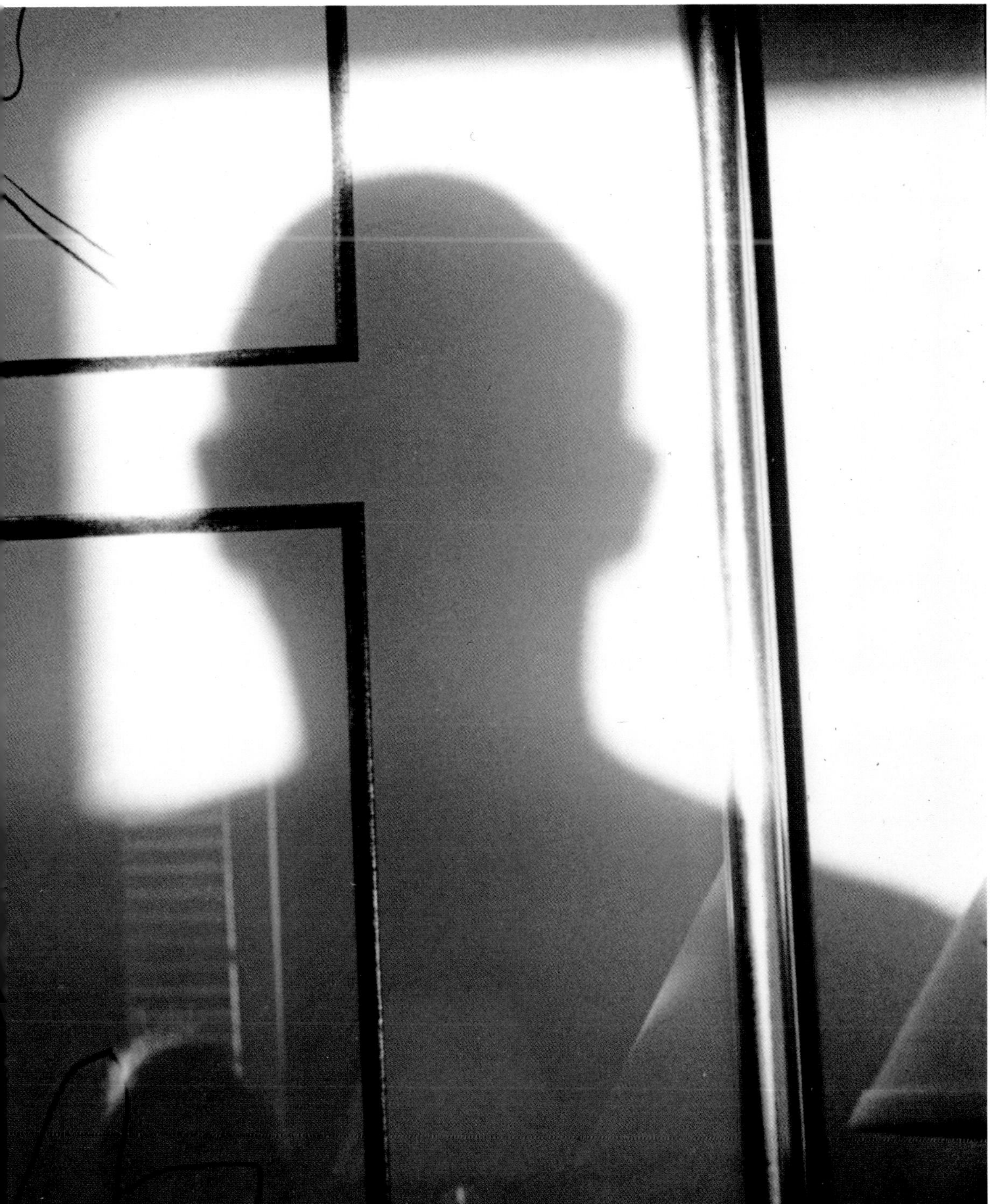

reaffirm the presence of you

of me

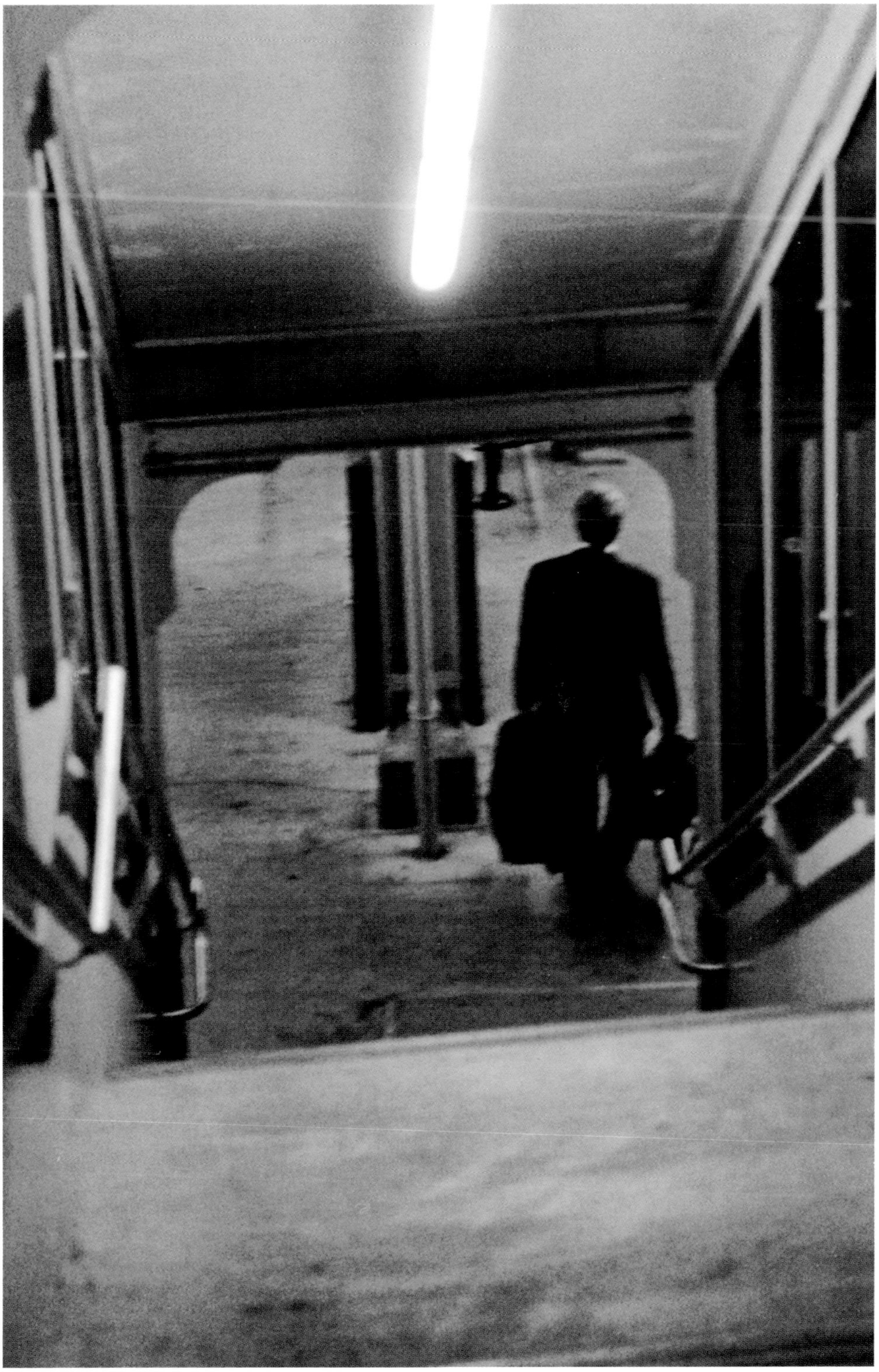

the beauty I see is seeing,
its wonder, its pity

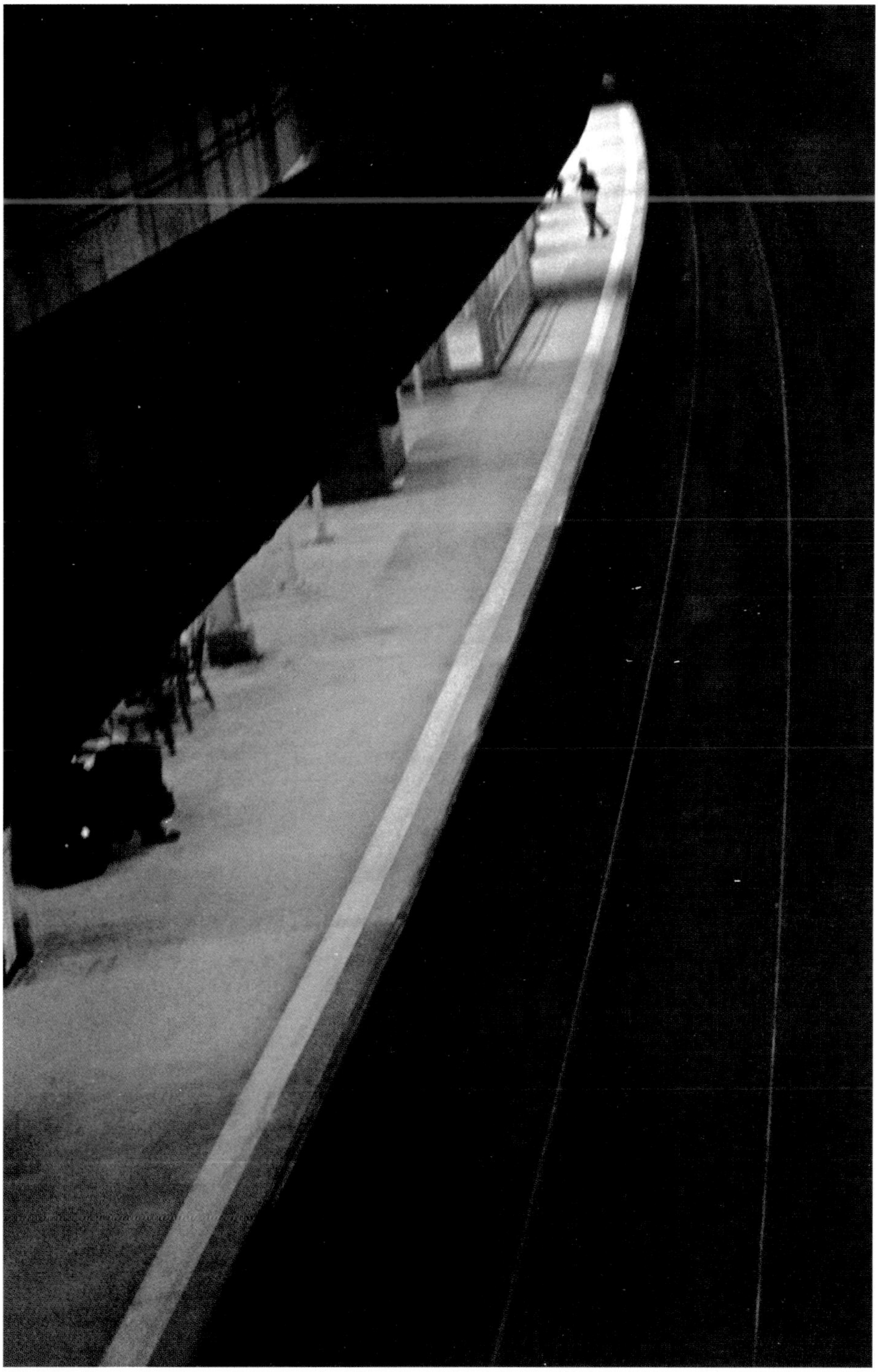

yesterday's rain, today's sun
clouds unfold gently
kissed by a rainbow

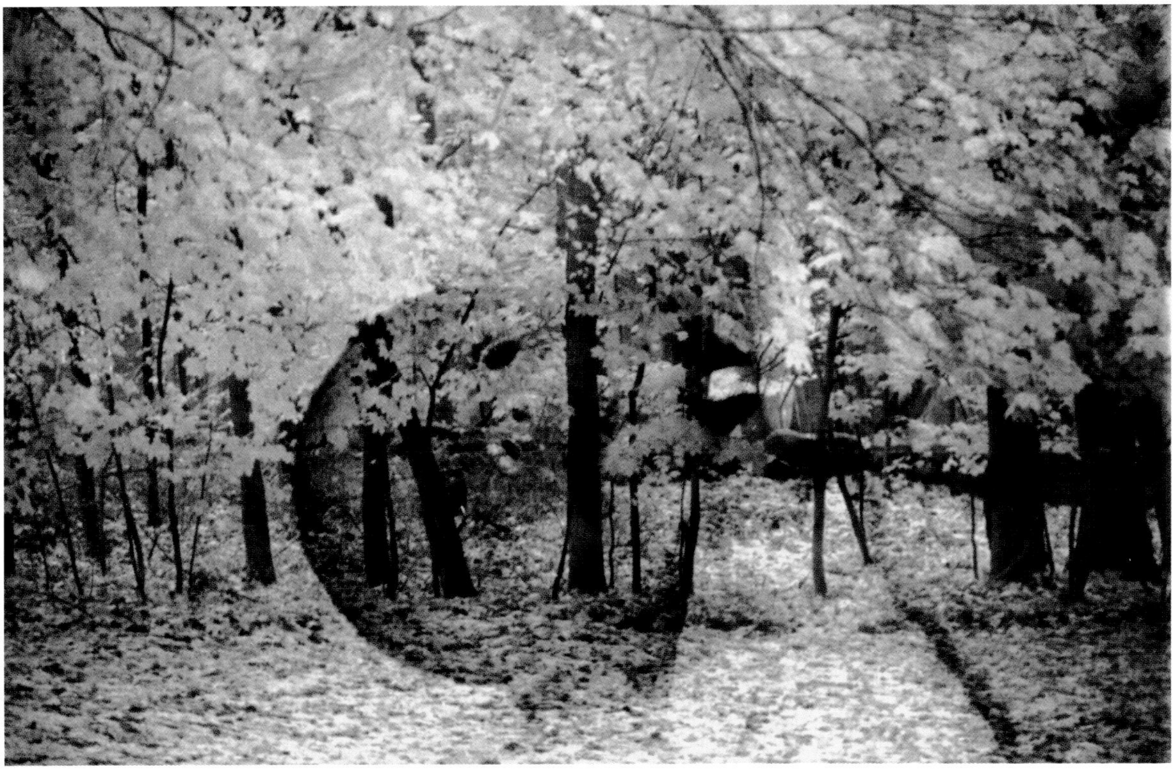

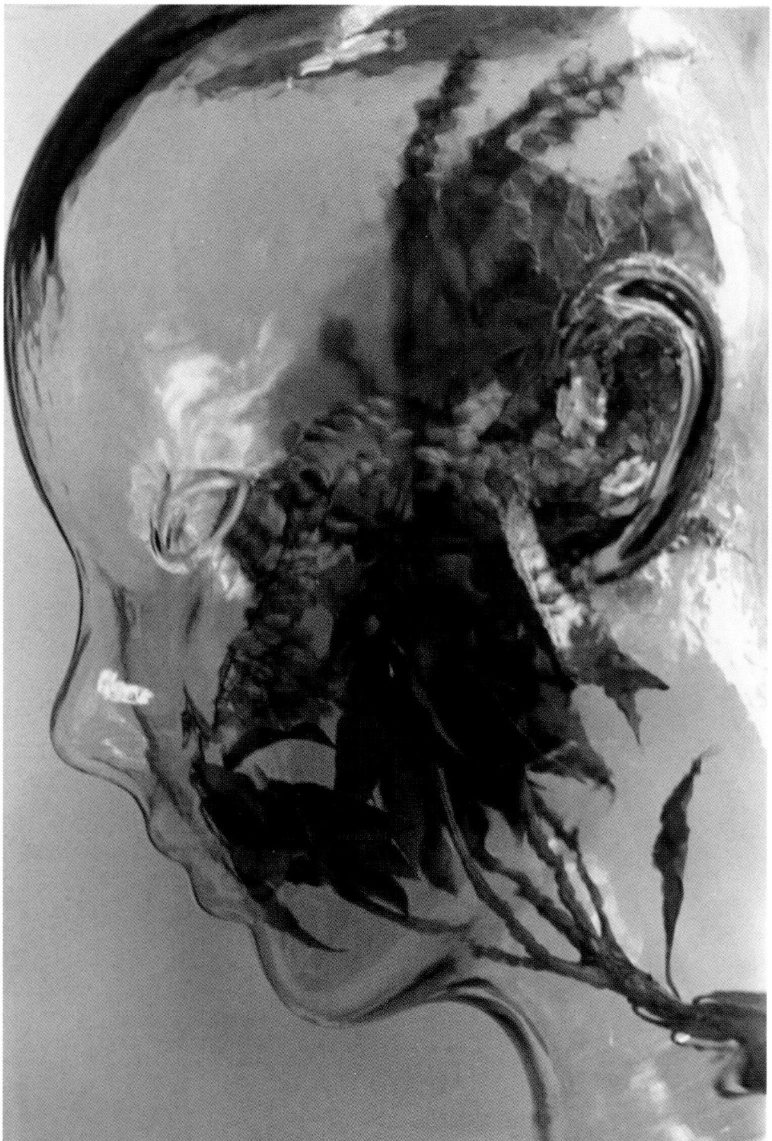

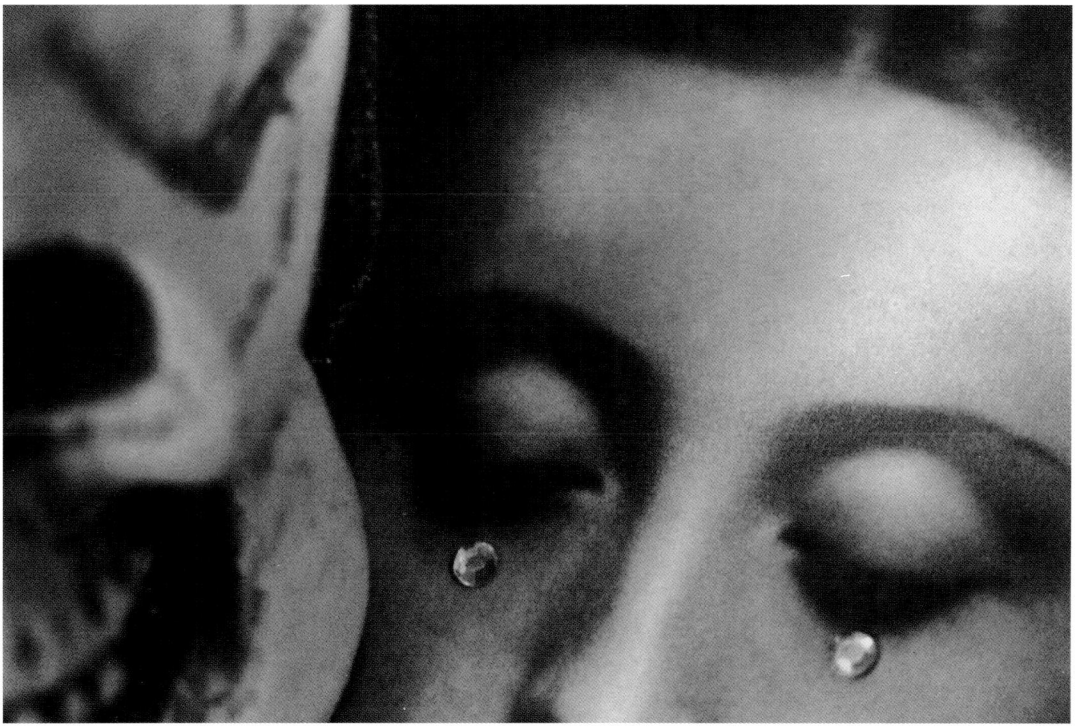

remembering with closed eyes

moments inside me

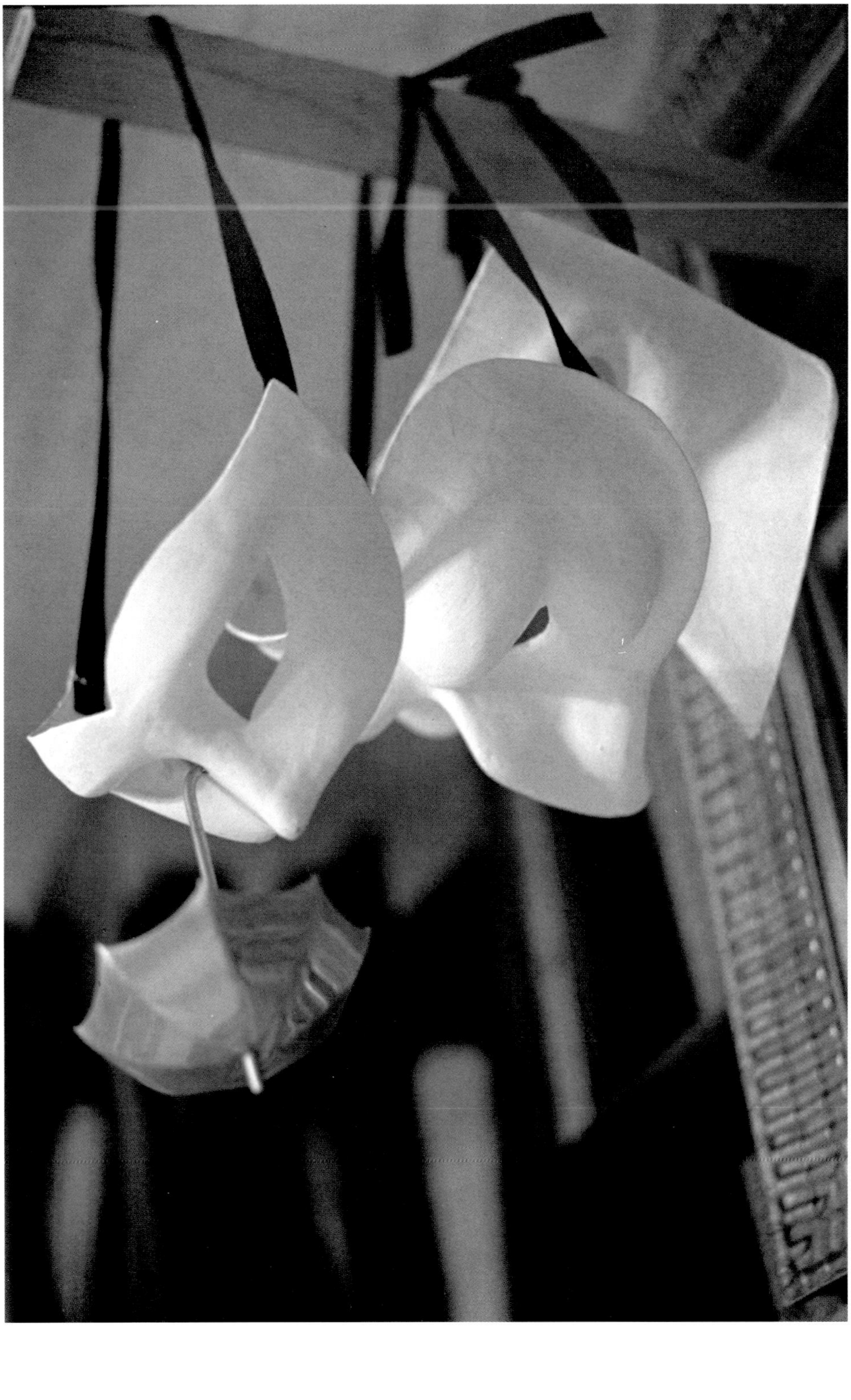

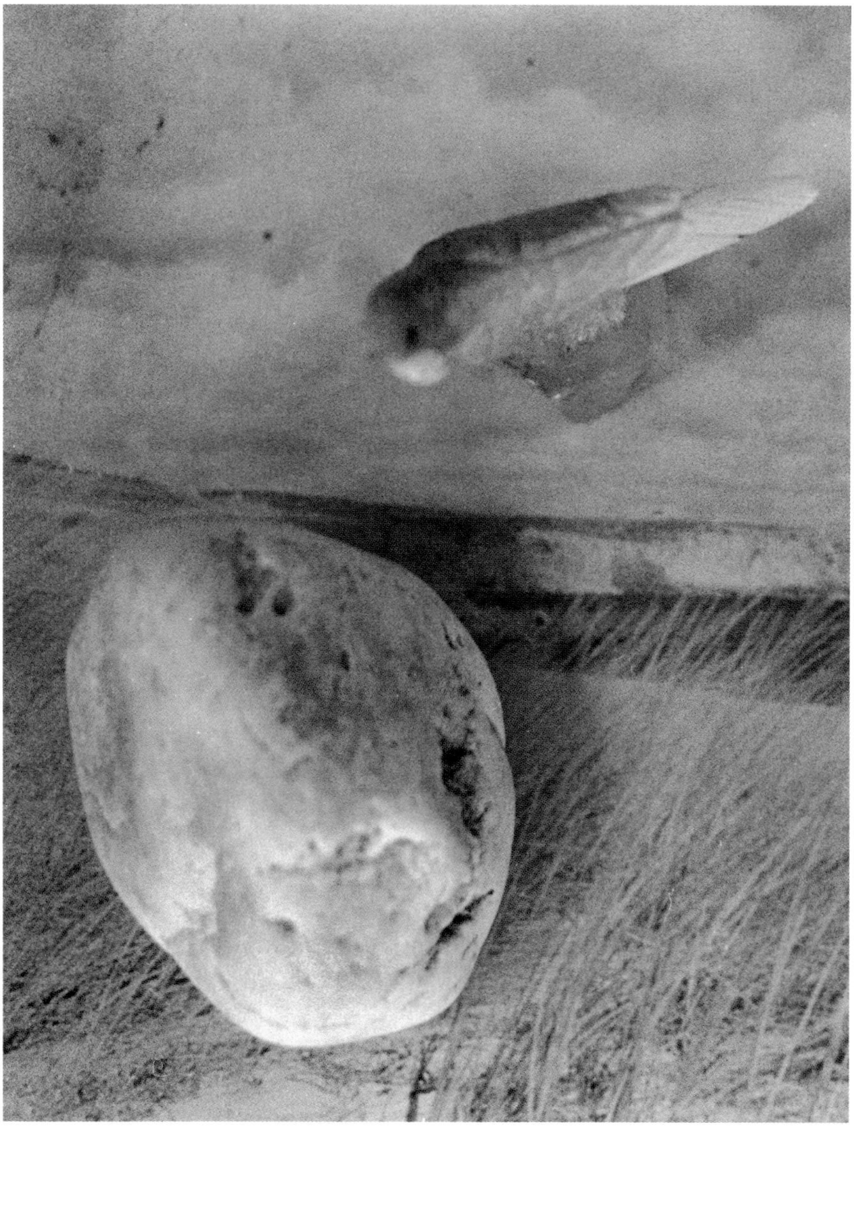

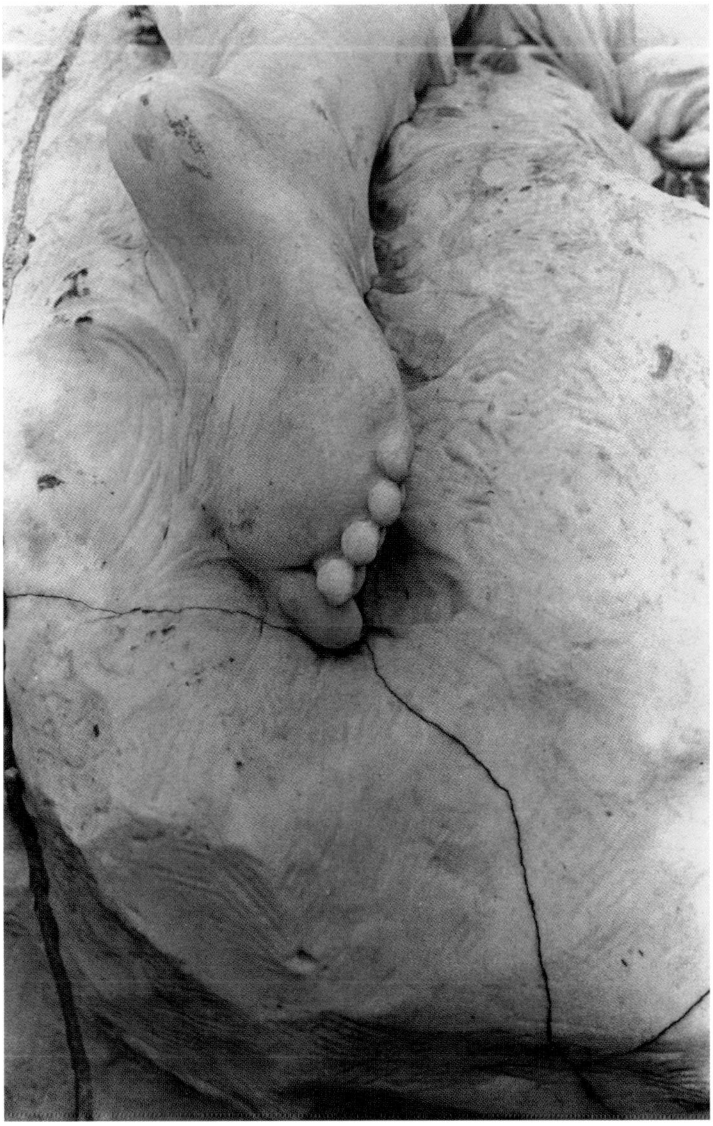

the ending beauty
of today's memory

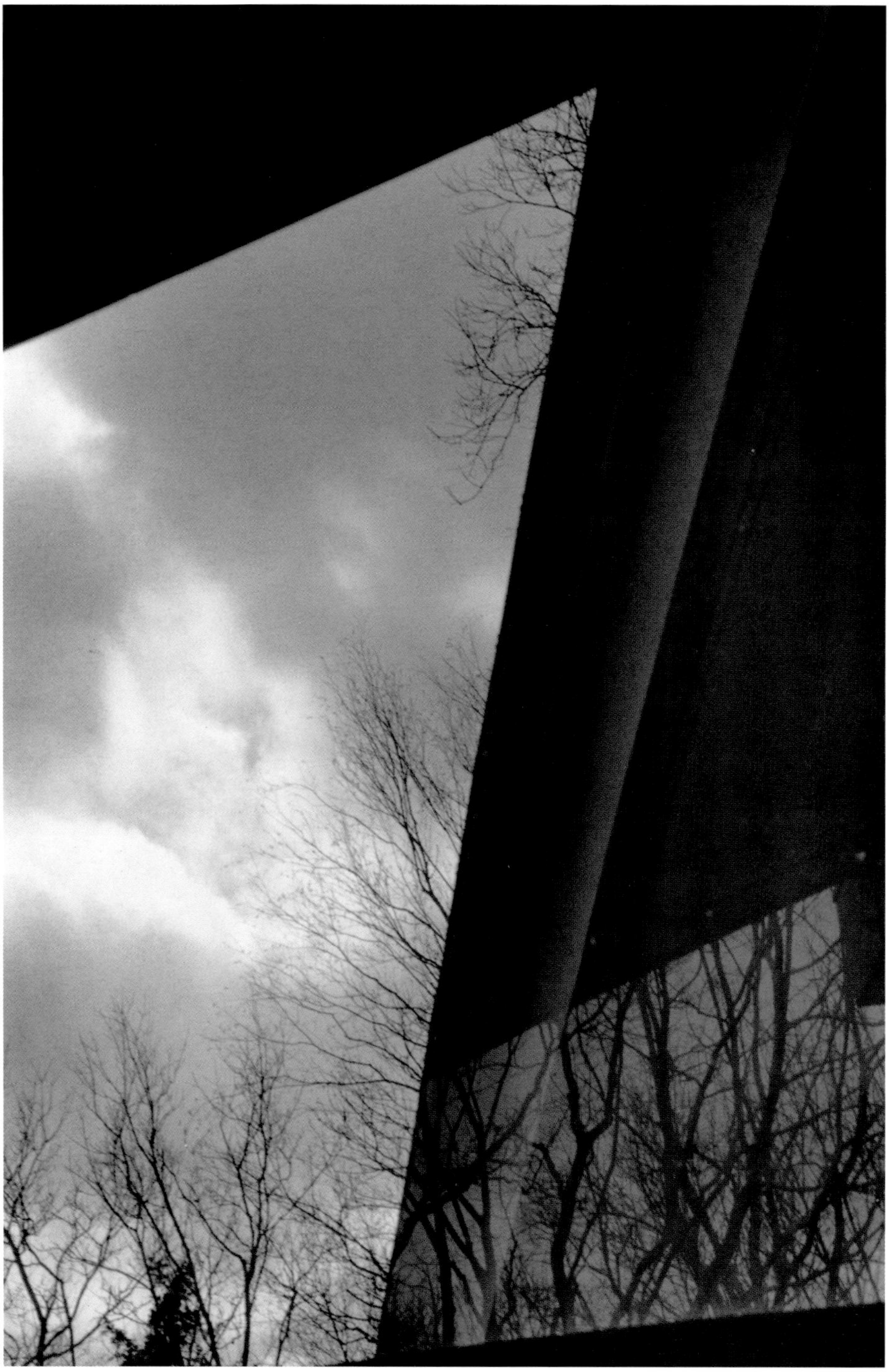

tomorrow not promised
light and shadow continue

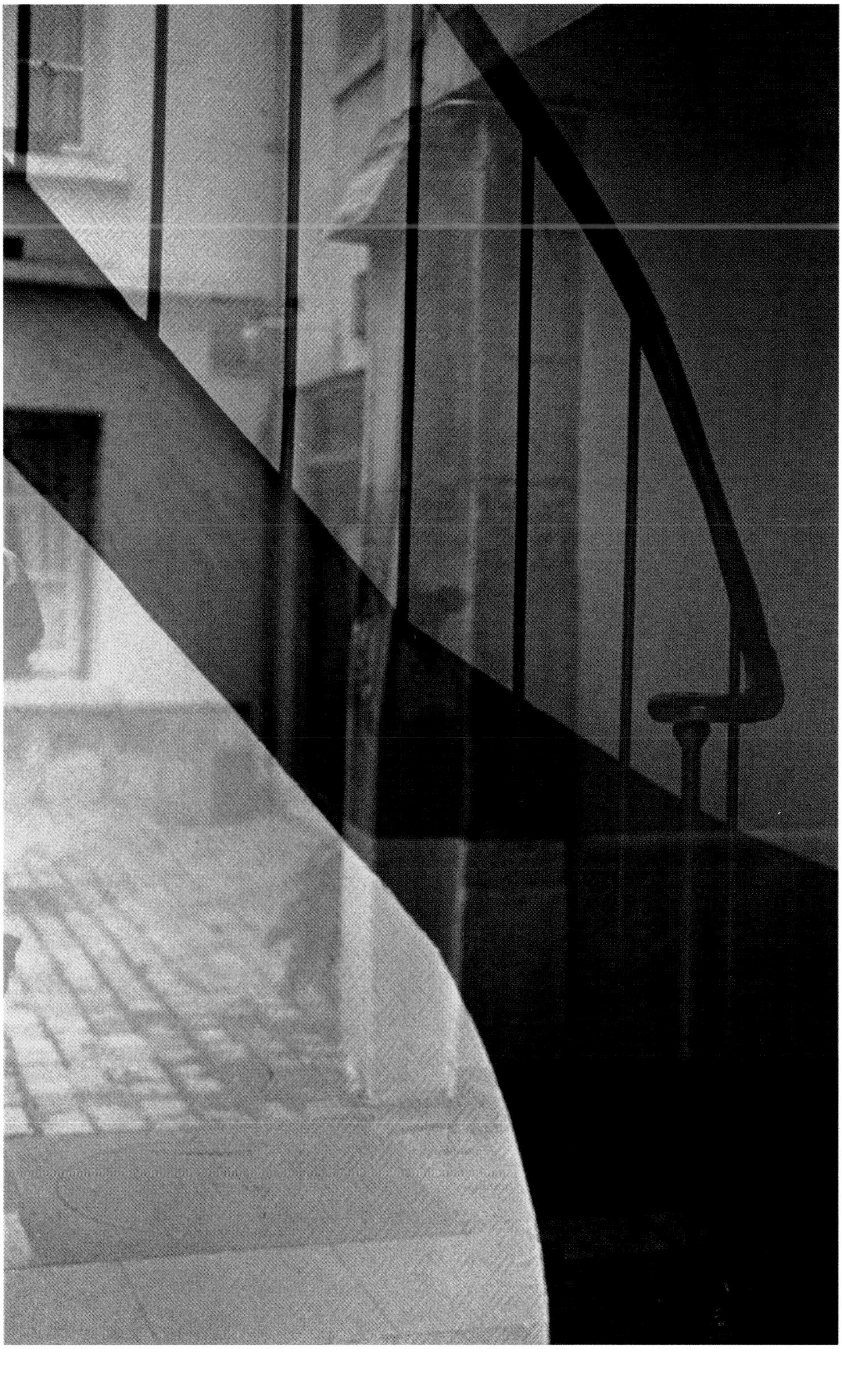

embracing life's dream,
eyes and heart open
accepting the treasured gift
life

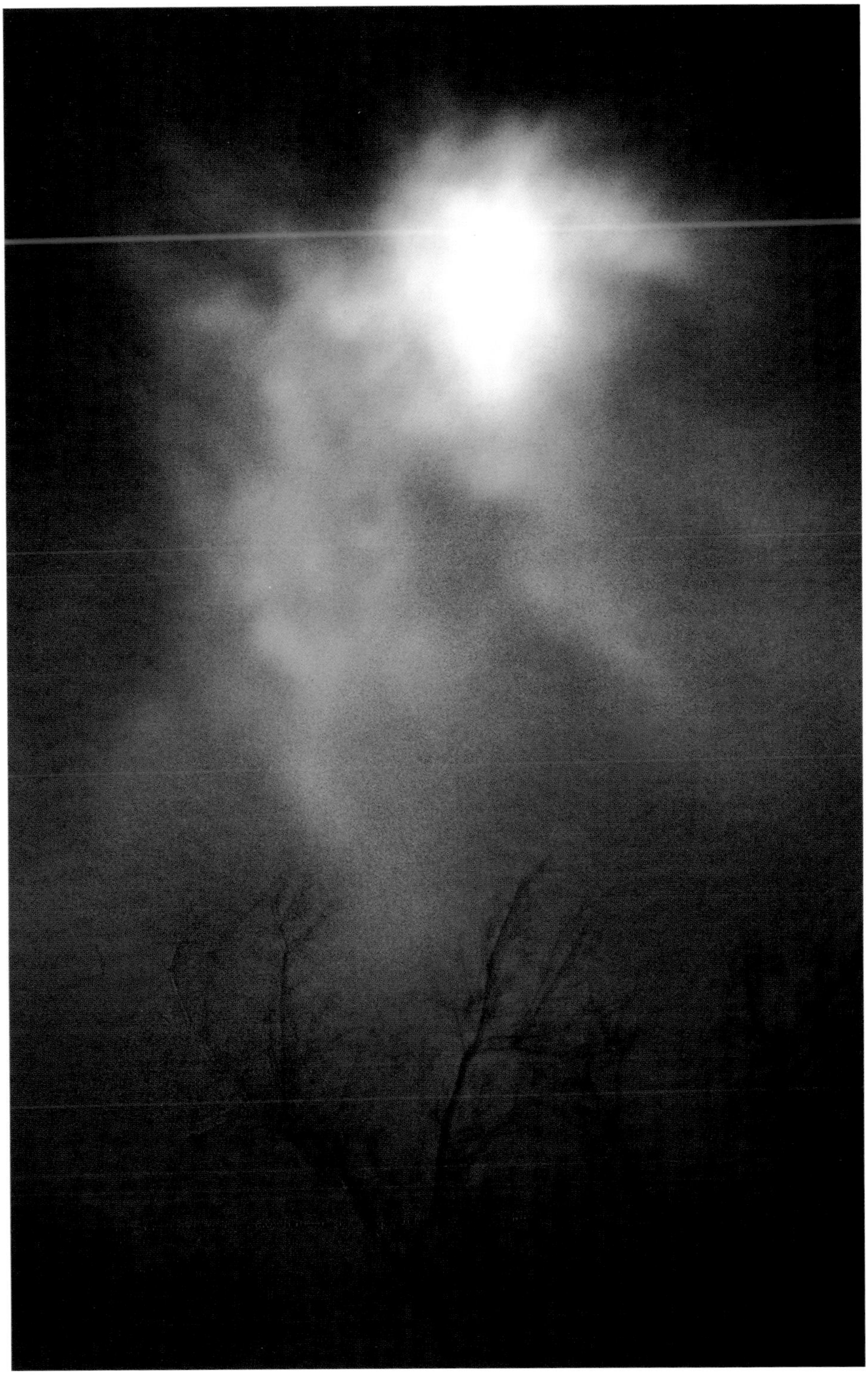

hurrying slowly
a new day begins.

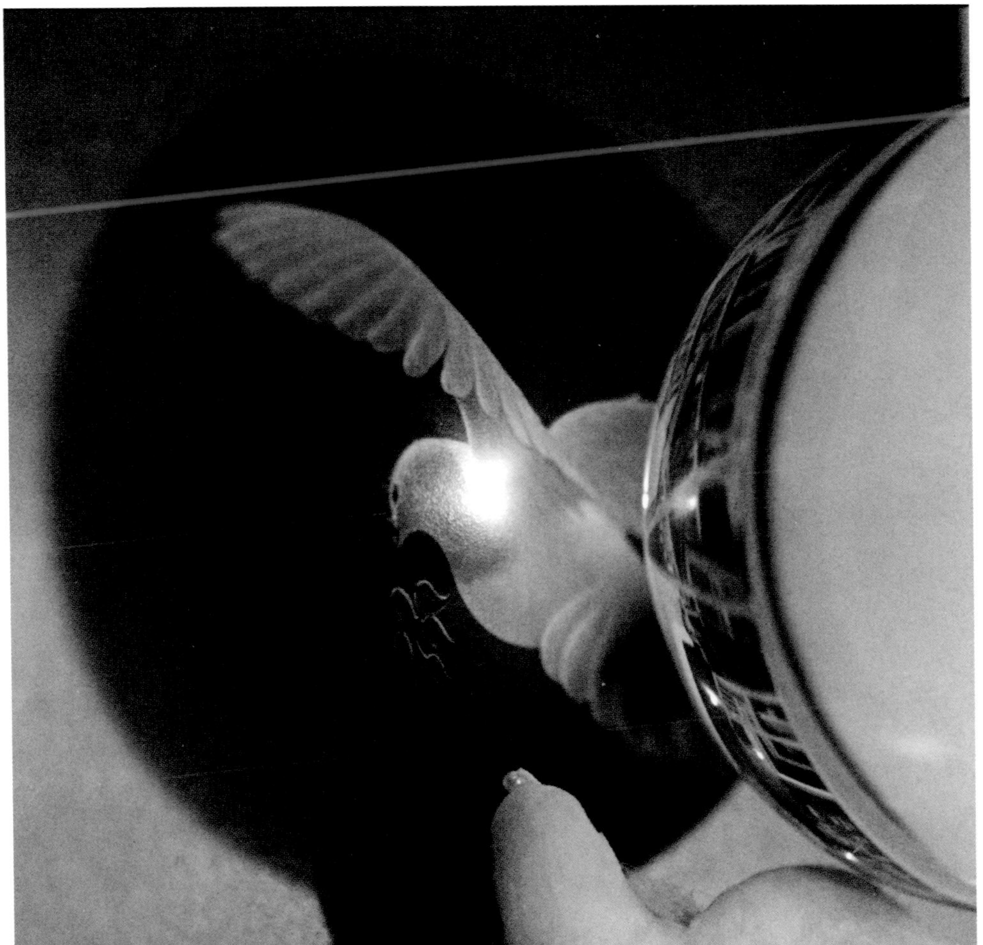

LIFE'S DREAM

by Claire Yaffa

Our dream of life will end, as dreams do
a flower lasting a short time before a petal falls
leaves touching before breaking apart
embraced by the wind
whispering who we are
words unspoken at life's end
never wanting to say good-bye
we wonder at the mystery surrounding our lives
to our sense of pity, beauty and pain,
the latent feeling of fellowship with all creation...
the loneliness of innumerable hearts
to the solidarity in dreams, in joy,
in sorrow, in aspirations
in illusions, in hope,
in fear which binds men to each other,
which binds together all humanity –
the dead to the living
*and the living to the unborn.**
days are almost gone before they arrive
the moon gives light to my shadow,
the minor of myself I see
watching you
watching me.
your eyes are mine
disappearing reflections
reaffirm the presence of you
of me
the beauty I see is seeing,
its wonder, its pity
yesterday's rain, today's sun
clouds unfold gently
kissed by a rainbow
remembering with closed eyes
moments inside me
the ending beauty
of today's memory
tomorrow not promised
light and shadow continue
embracing life's dream,
eyes and heart open
accepting the treasured gift
life
hurrying slowly
a new day begins.

*Joseph Conrad, "The Nigger of Narcissus"

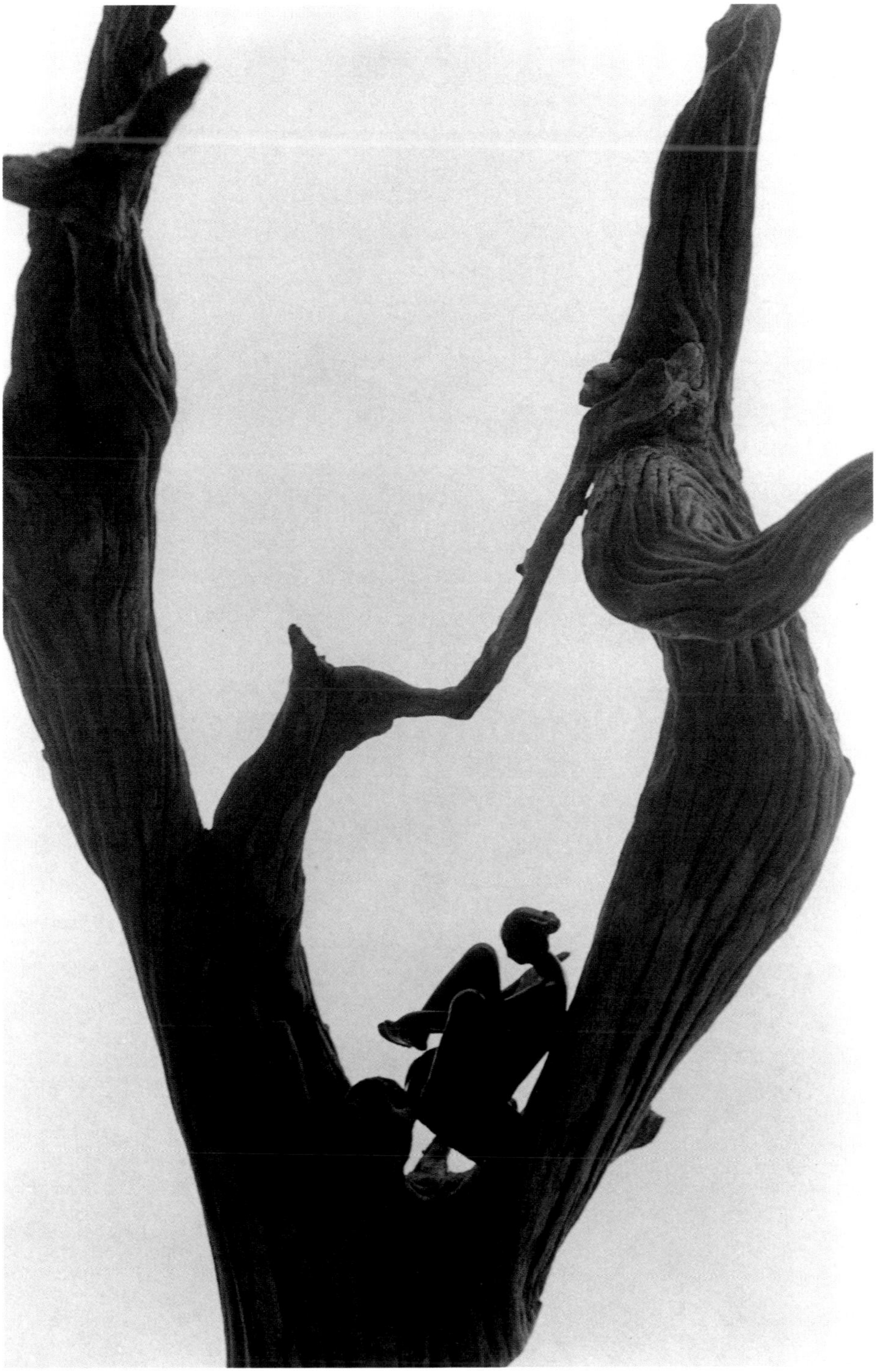

List of plates

Page 55: Bedford, New York/ June 2004

Page 56: Paris, France/ February 2002

Page 57: Bedford, New York/ October 2004

Page 59: Bedford, New York / March 2006

Page 60-61: Bedford, New York/ July 2005 (My mother's family)

Page 63: Mount Kisco, New York/ June 2005

Page 65: Florida/ October 2005

Page 67: New York City/ January 2004

Page 68: Bedford, New York/ April 2006 (My father's books)

Page 69: Bedford, New York/ November 2005 (My brother)

Page 71: Bedford, New York/ March 2005

Page 72-73: Beverly Hills, California/ February 2006 (My husband, Dick)

Page 75: Katonah, New York/ August 2005

Page 77: Katonah, New York/ August 2005

Page 79: Bedford, New York/ April 2004

Page 80: Bedford, New York/ May 2006

Page 81: Bedford, New York/ October 2005

Page 83: Mamaroneck, New York/ January 2005

Page 84: Bedford, New York/ October 2005

Page 85: Paris, France/ November 2004

Page 87: Bedford, New York/ August 2005

Page 88: Bedford, New York/ March 2006

Page 89: Bedford, New York/ August 2005

Page 91: Paris, France/ November 2004

Page 93: Bedford, New York/ January 2005

Page 95: Bedford, New York/ March 2005

Page 99: Bedford, New York,/ July 2005

Exhibitions

Leica and Other Photographers
Ongoing project

The Human Face of the Homeless
Ongoing project

Obscura Gallery,
Denver, CO
2007
Life's Dream and Other Photographs
Exhibition

Aperture at 50: Photography Past/Forward
2006
Group exhibition/traveling exhibition

Katonah Museum: Hot Pics
2006
Juried exhibition

The Vincent J. Fontana Center
for the Prevention of Child Abuse
New York, NY
2005
Permanent collection

Chelsea Art Museum, New York, NY
December 2003
Celebration of Women
Group exhibition [Publication, Assouline]

Fait et Cause, Paris, France
June 2002
Life & Death Once Upon A Time: Children with AIDS

Simon Wiesenthal Center
@ Art Director's Club, New York, NY
1999
Who Will Remember?
Holocaust survivors, rescuers, hidden children

Office of the Westchester County Executive,
White Plains, NY
December 1998
Homeless children

Rye Art Center, Rye, NY
October 1998
Through The Lens
Juried exhibition of Westchester artists

International Center of Photography,
New York, NY
September 1998
Light and Shadow

Camera Obscura Gallery, Denver, CO
August 1998
Light and Shadow
Neuberger Museum, Harrison, NY
December 1996
Children with AIDS
Lecture and exhibition

Neuberger Museum, Harrison, NY
Summer 1996
Harrison Mosaic: Portraits of Citizens Living in Harrison, New York
Lecture and exhibition

Cleveland Museum of Health and Science,
Cleveland, OH
June-August 1995
Children with Aids: An Endangered Species

Rockland Center for Holocaust Studies, Inc.
Spring Valley, NY
1994
Who Will Remember?

Sarah Lawrence College, Bronxville, NY
1993
Children With Aids: An Endangered Species

Camera Obscura Gallery, Denver, CO
1992
A Dying Child is Born: The Story of Tracy
Katonah Museum, Katonah, NY
1992
The Concerned Artist
Juried exhibition

The Bridge Gallery, White Plains, NY
1992
Remembering Together: Photodocumentary of Survivors Rescuers and Hidden Children of the Holocaust
The Bridge Gallery, White Plains, NY
1992
Making A Difference
Portraits of homeless children and families at summer camp

Nardin Gallery, Katonah, NY
1992
Juried show

Hiram Halle Memorial Library, Pound Ridge,NY
1992
A Dying Child is Born: The Story of Tracy

Nikon House, New York, NY
1991
A Photographic Mosaic
Juried exhibition

Sarah Lawrence College, Bronxville, NY
1990
Discovery: A Continuing Journey

New York Foundling Hospital, New York, NY
1989 to present
Permanent collection, lobby

American Academy of Pediatrics, Chicago, IL
1989 to present
Portraits of Children
Permanent collection

The Bridge Gallery, White Plains, NY
1988
Homeless in Westchester County

The White Plains Museum Gallery, White Plains, NY
1988
Homeless in Westchester County

The International Center of Photography, New York, NY
1987
Reaching Out
The problems of child abuse and rehabilitation

Sarah Lawrence College, Bronxville, NY
1987
Our World, Photographs of Children

Harrison Public Library, Harrison, NY
1982
The Story of A Life, Mrs. Mosher

The United Nations, New York, NY
1979
The International Year of The Child
Exhibition and poster

White Plains Museum Gallery, White Plains, NY
1979
The Child
For 'The International Year of the Child'

The Hudson River Museum, Yonkers, NY
1977
The Blue Hammer: Portraits of Children at LeakeWatts Children's Home
One woman exhibition

Mexico
1975
International Year of the Woman Conference
Poster and invitation

Harrison Public Library, Harrison, NY
1972
Portraits of Children

Ms. Yaffa's photographs have appeared in *The New York Times, Food Patch, Woman's News, Vogue, The Wag, Vanity Fair, Daily News, Newsday, NBC News, ABC News.*

She was the recipient of the 1995 Council for The Arts Award for "Outstanding Artist in Westchester County."

Publications

LEICA Photographers and others
Exhibition and Book, in progress
2007

The Human Face of the Homeless
Exhibition and Forum
2007

Divertissement
To be published 2008

Moments
Ruder Finn Press
2005

Embracing the Past:
"The Elders Speak"
2004
[On aging]

History of The New York
Foundling Hospital
2001

Light and Shadow
APERTURE
1998

A Dying Child is Born:
The Story of Tracy
1990

Reaching Out
[The problems of
child abuse and rehabilitation]
1987

Homeless in Westchester County
1988

Biography

B.A. Sarah Lawrence College
1962

Research Technician
Memorial Sloan Kettering Hospital
1959-1966

Emergency Medical Technician and
one of the founders of the
Harrison Volunteer Ambulance Corps
1983-1988

Photographic studies with:
Fred Picker, Lisette Model, Phillipe Halsman,
Ben Fernandez, W. Eugene Smith,
George Tice, Eva Rubinstein, Joseph
Schneider, Sean Kernan, Ralph Gibson,
Duane Michals, Cornell Capa, Gordon Parks
Photo Editor
Westchester Magazine
1977- 1987

Chairperson
Breadth of Vision, Fashion Institute of
Technology, NY
1975
[Largest juried exhibition of women's
photography in the United States]

Photography Coordinator
United Nations, NY
The International Woman's Arts Festival
1974